My UnHollywood Family

My UnHollywood Family

Robert Crane

Oregon Greystone Press
Portland, Oregon
2024

Copyright © 2024

All rights reserved. No part of this book may be reproduced, distributed, or transmitted in any form or by any means, including photocopying, recording or digital scanning, or other electronic or mechanical methods, without the prior written permission of the publisher and all authors, except in the case of brief quotations embodied in critical reviews and certain other noncommercial uses permitted by copyright law. For permission requests, please address Oregon Greystone Press.

First Edition 2024, published with Oregon Greystone Press.

This book is a work of nonfiction.

Edited by Theresa Griffin Kennedy.

Printed in the United States of America

ISBN 979-8-218-50834-0

Cover and interior design by Chris Miller Design.

For Eric, Ian, Meagan, and Frankie

Praise

"Hollywood" is more than just a neighborhood in Los Angeles. It is synonymous with illusion, facade, easy solutions to conflicts, and happy endings for troubled relationships. Growing up as the son of a famous television actor, Robert Crane (and his family) occasionally took part in reinforcing the deceptions of the Dream Factory. Now, with his brief memoir My (UnHollywood)Family, Crane, a veteran journalist, provides an unvarnished, straightforward account of his family over the last seventy-five years that reveals greater similarities with far more of us in the post-war era than any Hollywood contrivance.

~Andrew Erish, author of *Col. William N. Selig, the Man Who Invented Hollywood* and *Vitagraph: America's First Great Motion Picture Studio*

This intelligently written memoir about a painful upbringing in the margins of storied Hollywood will touch the hearts of many a reader. Passion, glitter, and, ultimately, heartbreak, propel Crane's account of growing up in the shadow of parental self-absorption.

~Suzy Vitello, author of *Bitterroot*

They're nameless until the final pages of Robert Crane's My (Un-Hollywood) Family, but we get it early on: this is the tale of the talented extrovert we've come to know as television's "Hogan's Heroes" star Bob Crane and the tangled trail of wives and children he left behind when he was brutally murdered in 1978. The author, son of the TV star, lays it all out there—from his dad's sex addiction, his deer-in-the-headlights mother and "Nazi, with breasts" stepmother to the loving real estate agent stepfather who "saved" the family. An unblinking probe of family skeletons, Crane's compelling tale yet brims with love. Well, except for the stepmother.

~Joseph B. Atkins, author of *Harry Dean Stanton: Hollywood's Zen Rebel*

Robert Crane has led an extraordinary life in and around the glittering cauldron better known as Hollywood. He's told the tale of his less than typical upbringing in various venues, but never quite so powerfully or with such raw intensity as he has in his all-too-real, dark family story, "My UnHollywood Family." Robert's fascinating deep dive into the many challenges he faced growing up as the son of the popular but troubled TV star, Bob Crane, better known to millions as Col. Hogan in "Hogan's Heroes," is as well-written as it is truly unnerving. Robert takes the reader on an emotional roller coaster through his and his family's many difficult experiences, not the least of which being Bob Crane's brutal, untimely demise in Scottsdale, Arizona. "My UnHollywood Family" traverses the rocky shoals of Robert's familial relationships and the lifelong impact his larger-than-life father had on him, his Mother, and siblings. Fortunately, he found his way through it all to become a respected interviewer and outstanding writer. It's our good fortune that Robert Crane is able to translate so much personal heartache and trauma into a work that is such an eminently accessible great read.

~Steve Cuden, host of the *StoryBeat* podcast

Robert David Crane stands emotionally naked for all the world to see in his latest book, *My UnHollywood Family* in which we get to meet the branches of the family tree that weren't on TV, radio, tabloid cover pages or found bludgeoned to death..

As his father, Bob Crane did during his meteoric rise in the 1960s entertainment world, Robert David Crane, similarly, in his memoir-ish tone, shoots from the hip, off the cuff, no script, in a total stream of consciousness. The difference between his father's shtick and Robert's is the difference between comedy and tragedy. Bob Crane made us laugh, until he didn't. Robert David Crane makes us weep, until… Closure?

Read *My UnHollywood Family* if you really want to know where you came from, what you're made of and how you will handle the thing that is just one untimely phone call away.

~Joe Coyle
Writer, Actor, Producer

It's clear that Bob Crane's upbringing was not your typical first generation Baby Boomer model, but then, every family has their own story. I want to know how he made it out in one piece. Crane is obviously a keen observer with a great memory. He takes on the institution of marriage and anguishes over a father who never really grew up, and parents that dared not express-their true feelings. I think we all can connect with pieces of how he and his sisters waded through this minefield, but Crane interjects just the right amount of humor to make this journey entertaining. Oh, and I think the stepmom was capable of anything, including murder.

~John Cerney, large-scale artist

Acknowledgements

Thank you Theresa Griffin Kennedy and Leslie Bertram Crane for reading various drafts and offering expert notes.

Also by Robert Crane

Beyond Where the Buses Run: Stories

Hollywood Plateau

Two Friends Over Drinks

Boom! The Baby Boomer Album

Crane: Sex, Celebrity, and My Father's Unsolved Murder

Bruce Dern: A Memoir

Jack Nicholson: The Early Years

My Life as a Mankiewicz

Burn the Ice

No Stone Unturned

SCTV: Behind the Scenes

My UnHollywood Family

"A dead man is the best fall guy in the world. He never talks back."

~ Raymond Chandler

Introduction

June 29, 1978 will live on in the mind of one man indefinitely.

It remains a date burned upon his brain. In the mind of a young man who had just celebrated his 27th birthday two days before — Robert David Crane — the oldest child and oldest son of actor and radio personality, Bob Crane, this date will never leave his consciousness, and can never be forgotten. It is the date of his father's murder, the day the life of celebrated and beloved TV actor and star of Hogan's Heroes, Bob Crane, was destroyed by an awkward and ungainly man. A man dominated by envy and a desire for revenge, John Carpenter, a man who in my opinion got away with premeditated murder.

Now, this once young man wants to set the record straight about the experiences he cannot forget, the losses that shaped him, and that continue their forward moving dark energy, where "closure" becomes an alluring falsehood, a tease and the most elegant and expansive of lies.

This book represents a reckoning with the past. Robert Crane shares memories of that past and his disturbed and sociopathic stepmother, Patti Olsen/Sigrid Valdis/Patricia Crane. She was a sinister woman who guarded her secret agendas well, a woman who inexplicably called herself a "Humanist" when she was anything but humanist in her approach to those people she pushed herself on, tormented and stole from.

Patti knew of John Carpenter's existence, and it is not unthinkable that she lured Carpenter into a secret alliance. As she was someone who vigilantly monitored all those close to Bob Crane, it would have been simple and in her best interest to contact Carpenter. She may also have encouraged his resentment of Bob Crane, encouraging the idea that Crane used Carpenter and unfairly discarded him. It would have been easy for Patti, very easy, to do all these things because perpetrating betrayal was what she did best in life.

And even after death, Patti orchestrated betrayal.

Using a pen to excavate the fragments of a life can be daunting, painful and also strangely freeing. Author Robert David Crane is familiar with that process and in this book he shares in a taut, frank and stark tone, what happened all those decades ago when a siren came upon his parents and sacrificed one of them to the flames of her troubled inner life.

Patti often sat alone at a kitchen nook - in a home purchased with Bob Crane's money - a cigarette in one hand and an endlessly filled wine glass in the other. There were no lights on as the purple shadows of evening gathered. All a young Robert Crane could see was the red burning ember of his stepmother's cigarette, her face enveloped in darkness, her shrouded form, closed in upon itself, silent, unyielding, revealing nothing.

One thing readers will lament most with My UnHollywood Family is that the book is not longer. And there will be questions - countless questions - for its author - who wants people to remember that it was his stepfather, Chuck Sloan who saved his family. *"My stepfather took the baton from my father and cleared his own path. My father had failed my family, and then Chuck created his own path and salvaged what he could."*

Oregon Greystone Press is honored to share this historically important recounting of the timeless machinations of an American life. The love destroyed, a parent murdered, innocence lost, and those who are left behind, who are able and willing to persevere, pick up the pieces and make the best of what they have left, with Robert Crane's mother, *Anne*, the sole surviving, last "parent" standing.

Theresa Griffin Kennedy

My UnHollywood Family

> *"I enjoy life. That doesn't mean I don't care."*
> ~ Bob Crane

I was three years old and living with my mother and father in a brick apartment complex inhabited by working-class families in Bridgeport, Connecticut. One day I was sent on a mission: get the attention of the loud, tall, Italian woman living next door and bring her to our bathroom where my mother shriveled, bent over in excruciating pain.

Decades later, I would find out that my mother was in the throes of a miscarriage. This is the first memory I have that I can recall.

My mother's mother was a Swedish immigrant from Helsingborg and her father was Armenian by way of Turkey.

My grandmother had an uncle living in the United States who suggested that the younger members of the family join the search for the American Dream.

My grandmother was set to sail the Atlantic with two sisters when the sisters contracted diphtheria and eventually died. So, my grandmother decided to make the journey alone. My grandfather and his brother and cousin escaped the 1915 Armenian Genocide and met other cousins in New York. Most of my other family members were not so lucky, and perished.

My grandparents met at the home of a well to do family in Tuxedo Park, New York, where my grandmother was a uniform-wearing domestic and my grandfather was a chauffeur.

They fell in love, left and married. Soon, two daughters were born two years apart.

My grandmother watched over her young daughters at the home front in Stamford, Connecticut, while her husband worked as a tailor. My mother looked Swedish with a fair complexion and reddish-blonde hair. Her sister was darker-skinned with black hair.

My father's mother's family was Russian and his father's side originated from England. I never heard how my grandparents met, only that my grandmother's family lived on the wrong side of the tracks, so to speak, as opposed to my grandfather's family, with their middle-class upbringing.

Decades later, I would find out my grandmother was a high school dropout and a cervical cancer survivor. They were forced into marriage when my grandmother became pregnant with my father's older brother. They also resided in Stamford, Connecticut, where my grandmother took care of her sons while her husband worked as a furniture salesman.

My father absorbed the Russian side with early photographs reflecting a distinctive Asian construct to his eyes. My grandparents loved my father. He could do no wrong. My grandfather barely tolerated his oldest son. Later, there would be shouting matches between father and son and plenty of alcohol consumed.

My mother took care of me and never held an official job because my father was never home, but always "working." He liked to entertain people. He liked to make an audience laugh. He played the drums with different bands at night and worked at a jewelry store by day. He continually sent out resumes and audiotapes to local radio stations.

Finally, he got a job at a radio station in Hornell, New York, as a custodian/staff announcer. When reading drab copy, he would find ways to work in his sense of humor. Working at a station in Bristol, Connecticut, was more of the same but the all-important word "experience" was in play.

Later, as a teenager, I couldn't grapple with the needed experience. I wanted it now. My father explained as best he could that experience involved time – days, months, years, sometimes, decades, sometimes, lifetimes – to achieve goals, and, sometimes, never. My father honed his craft – playing popular music, teasing sponsors and their commercials with sound effects, his great voice and off-the-wall banter.

My father made thousands of friends he never met and a few he did. He was expected to be a salesman like his father but he rebelled against the common ground expectations, and wanted to go higher with his own voice. Laughter and the unexpected story drove him. In some languages, "ambition" equates to the trauma of separation.

My mother focused on her young child, watching over me as I played with my girlfriend in a small, metal jeep with pump pedals, darting down sidewalks through the staid, apartment city. My mother had no discernible skills except for playing the glockenspiel in the high school band and the piano at home. Her cooking included meat and potatoes, and canned vegetables.

But, she was my mother first and she loved me.

Neither set of grandparents celebrated anything, it seemed. On my mother's side, her parents behaved as if their papers would be confiscated and they would be returned to their native countries if they splurged on any kind of celebration or spur-of-the-moment fun.

Every birthday, every wedding, every anniversary was celebrated in a low-budget, quiet, reflective manner. My father's parents were born in the United States but also managed to keep emotions down. His father's idea of cutting loose was to come home from a day's work, turn on the record player to easy-listening band music, light up a cigarette, and pour a glass of bourbon. He would let my grandmother know when he was ready to sit down to dinner.

The idea of his youngest son not pursuing a career in sales baffled and disturbed my grandfather. My grandmother being a high school dropout was a bit more open to her son breaking the family expectations. My grandfather's side of the family expected more – a name, a reputation among the small-town hoi polloi.

Money was always an issue – coming up with the mortgage payment each month, feeding the family, filling up the gas tank, riding the bus, setting aside extra change for an ice cream or a movie. When my parents asked my grandfather for a loan to buy a Coldspot Refrigerator, my grandfather resisted in no uncertain terms until my father retreated and called off the ask. He/my parents would take care of it on his/their own.

It taught my father an important lesson: do not rely on anyone. Do it yourself. His life was now shaped and defined as a lone wolf: succeeding and failing, living and dying on his own terms.

A career in radio and music was not on the radar of either side of the family. This mass of energy attracted and repelled my mother to my father – she liked but was envious of the energy force that was her husband's greatest attribute. He was a glass bubbling over; she was a glass half-filled, always threatening to run on empty. The enthusiasm was never present for my mother. I never saw her bound out of bed in the morning, cook breakfast, deliver the day's schedule, get in the car, and take us on an adventure; whereas, every day was an unrehearsed, unscripted adventure for my father. My mother was her mother. My father rejected the notion, in any way, of replicating *his* father.

Unlike playing the drums, he didn't practice radio hosting; he just jumped in never knowing where he'd land. The act was more exciting than selling a watch or a ring or a dining room table or a boxspring and mattress. As my father relied on himself more and more and garnered small successes – experience – his wife and his parents became less involved, less opinionated.

My father was his own creation and no one would block his path.

The refrigerator was paid for; that pleased my mother but that was nothing. My father wanted more than small-town thinking. He wanted no expectations, no rules from his family. The purchase was a beacon of light for him. My father proved to himself that he didn't need and couldn't rely on anyone but himself. He had shifted into a higher gear and was moving too fast for my mother. My father shifted his posture. Instead of looking down or straight ahead – status quo - he started to look up. He wanted New York where his heroes like Arthur Godfrey and Steve Allen ruled the airwaves and Frank Sinatra and Buddy Rich ruled live theatre stages.

My mother took me to Beardsley Park and the Zoo on a regular basis with a side visit to a wonderfully greasy hamburger stand – I can smell it but I can't quite remember the name – was it Morokses? I enjoyed the zoo but couldn't wait to dive into one of those cheeseburgers, and French fries (with plenty of ketchup) and an ice cold Coca-Cola. An outing with my mother. Seeing the world at large! An experience to share with my father when he got home. I saw a giraffe that day and he didn't.

There were picnics with Armenian relatives – loud talk, laughter, playing with a bulldog. I was cute and said funny things and sounded English – "bahd" instead of "bird." My mother and I spent hours and hours together. I was her little entertainer that she still had control of. We would spend time with my grandmother who was now solo, her husband entering the hospital for an ulcer operation and never exiting, a victim of peritonitis at the age of only fifty-one.

There were no wrongful death lawsuits, no payouts from the doctors or hospital, no ambulance-chasing attorneys back then. My grandfather died and my grandmother buried him, it was just that simple. Life carried on. My grandmother was lost, sad, and depressed, though. Her only love and support was gone forever. There was no life insurance.

My grandmother eventually sold their modest home for $18,000. There was never any design on returning to Sweden, her motherland. She had two grown daughters with two son-in-laws and three grandchildren in the United States. And, she was not about to miss her favorite television program, "The Lawrence Welk Show."

My grandfather, mother and I had/have the same blood type: O negative.

My grandfather's passing created angst and turmoil for my mother and her sister. This was the beginning of life-long financial and housing support by the two sisters. The death resulted in my grandmother ping ponging back and forth between her daughters' residences.

My grandmother didn't exactly play with or read to me or my two cousins during stays, she wasn't that type of person. But she was a presence. The son-in-laws, however, grew tired of the lack of privacy and the continual payouts. My grandmother and mother even occasionally sparred verbally.

The elder had certain ideas about raising children and made comments about my father's often prolonged absences. My grandmother's facial expressions exhibited suspicion, anger or sadness when my father came up. But, when my grandmother let go and found a joke or throwaway line humorous, she would relax and cry with uncontrollable laughter. Those rare moments almost made up for the rest of the day.

Laughter was a rare commodity in the family. It was earned with sarcasm, a good joke, or an edgy attitude. My father's father would also lose it every so often – tears of joy. The person who unlocked the door, my father or me with something cute or precious I dreamed up to say, got points.

The grandparents soon listened to my father on the local Bridgeport radio station. His parents would comment on something funny that came out of his mouth or something he shouldn't have divulged over the airwaves involving his wife, mother, or mother-in-law. My father had recorded his mother's infectious laugh for use as a gag payoff and would have me on the air because of the absurdly cute observations and comments my four-year-old brain came up with.

I recorded singing the Borden's Milk theme song for use as a commercial spot on my father's program. I keep a 78rpm vinyl rendition of it to this day. Unplayable now but when I study the thickness of the record I can hear my innocent self singing, entertaining the locals but not necessarily the mad men of Madison Avenue.

My mother's mother was still trying to figure out how my father crawled into the audio box. My father would appear on local television from time to time and my grandmother really had a tough time with that concept. She actually peeked behind the television set once.

My father's wayward older brother was a World War Two veteran who had been burned as the result of an enemy attack on the aircraft carrier he served on. Unfortunately, no events during the rest of his life would prove as exciting as surviving an enemy bombing. He sold furniture like his father, smoked, drank, and thought he was the new crooner in town, the Tony Bennett of Stamford, Connecticut. He wore sunglasses indoors and often broke into laughter for no apparent reason.

My father periodically bailed him out of jail. Their mother cried as my grandfather shook his head in disappointment and poured another bourbon to take the edge off. The brothers were night and day, darkness and light. The difference in personalities produced conflict between them resulting in unwanted and unwarranted comments from the older sibling about my father's radio performance or drumming abilities. There was competition, rivalry, envy.

The lone wolf shell my father was building got harder and deflected negativity from any family member and the public at large. My father increased his speed and installed mental blinders. No sibling, no parent, would impede his single-mindedness to get out of Bridgeport and show the world a new energy force.

The more stamina my father displayed, the more my mother countered with lethargy. He wore her down with his career drive, his limitless ideas for radio programs and his latest goal to become an actor like his favorites – Jack Lemmon and Gig Young.

His optimism exhausted her.

My mother was used to a relatively calm and quiet home life as a child except when her mother would have a new fear or minor breakdown about dealing with the uncertainty of living her life in the United States, the rules, being accepted by her neighbors. My grandfather worried about the money aspect of survival but *that* changed upon his death.

I could see that my grandmother was lost without him. My mother and her sister contained the sadness and insecurity in their mother as best they could. My grandmother's biggest dream had been traveling to the United States and becoming a citizen although she would always be more Swedish than American. A husband and children had then followed.

There were no larger goals than the day-to-day paying the mortgage, preparing dinner, cleaning clothes, and attending to her daughters' needs. Why she was the only member of her family to leave Sweden I still don't know. Was she the true adventurer? Was she kicked out of the family? She and my mother did eventually sail to Sweden after my grandfather's death to visit relatives and friends.

Could she have been assessing the mood of the family for a permanent return? My mother didn't stray far from *her* mother's lifestyle – quiet celebrations, no ego, with the most important goal of getting through today. Life was in the here and now. My father was already planning on entering the highway at seventy-five miles an hour and exiting in the big city. My mother never had any goals more important than keeping her family together like her mother had done before her.

In time, an audition reel-to-reel ¼-inch audiotape featuring my father's sense of humor and timing made its way through CBS Radio New York to CBS Radio Los Angeles. The break. The opportunity. My parents were West Coast-bound in their Oldsmobile for a meeting with the station general manager and a scouting trip.

I stayed with my grandmother who was sensing changes in the family. She was not happy with the thought of her youngest daughter living three thousand miles away in the Wild West. She was the first in her immediate family to depart Scandinavia and now she was afraid that her daughter would be the first in the family to live on the opposite coast. Her fear came true. My father's interview with the powers that be went well and he secured a great radio job in the second largest media market in the country. It wasn't New York but it would do.

My parents found a rental home in the San Fernando Valley around the corner from the now iconic Casa Vega. We were so new to the area, we Easterners had no clue what Mexican food consisted of. They drove back to Bridgeport, packed the car with my father's clothing, he said his goodbyes and hit the highway again. Solo. My mother and I closed down the apartment and said our goodbyes. My mother booked Amtrak and she and her little boy left their security.

My father looked ahead (literally) and my mother looked back.

My father was on a mission and my mother was suddenly lost, the thought of being far away from her mother and sister provoked sadness and disorientation. My parents were in their mid-twenties and their world was tossed in the air.

My father welcomed the retreat from his small thinking family and a few friends. No more radio stations with dated equipment and small-time, local advertisers. Rather, there was a multi-story building with state-of-the-art professional equipment, spacious offices, and nation-wide sponsors, across the street from Columbia Studios in Hollywood, the same studio where Jack Lemmon and Gig Young filmed their movies.

My mother and I endured many days and nights on an uncomfortable train stopping in the worst parts of cities. Her mind was in Connecticut where she had her family, friends, Sunday picnics with our Armenian relatives, Beardsley Park, greasy hamburgers, dressing her son as George Washington for Halloween, snow, fun trips into New York City, Frank Sinatra at the Paramount Theatre, and accompanying my father to his drum lessons.

My mother loved my father, he made her laugh, and now he was moving their life together to the opposite side of the country. She followed with hesitation.

My mother and I stepped off the train at Union Station in downtown Los Angeles. We were tired but happy. We'd had enough of observing the backside of most cities and towns on the journey westward. Now, we saw tall buildings, City Hall, and freeways. My father was nowhere to be seen, though. My mother dialed both phone numbers she had for my father - a rental home in the San Fernando Valley and his work in Hollywood. No answer. We slowly moved our luggage curbside and hailed a cab for our new residence.

My father showed up that night. He had lost track of our arrival date. He was concentrating on being the new L.A. radio personality in the morning and promoting his show at Chambers of Commerce, Elks Lodges and anyone who would have luncheons with him, all over Los Angeles County.

Before the Ice Capades played the Pan Pacific Auditorium for their yearly Southern California visit, my father, mother and I were trained by a pretty professional ice skater for a five-minute act during intermission promoting this new Los Angeles radio personality, Bob Crane.

My father was funny, my mother was beautiful and I was just cute.

I don't remember anything about the brief interlude except that five minutes would be the only time my parents and I performed together. That was enough. By the way, no one fell.

My mother walked me to school every day passing that Mexican restaurant we never ate at - we were meat and potatoes, canned vegetables, and cold milk kind of people. Mexican, Chinese, and Japanese food were from another planet. We would have Italian occasionally but that was strictly spaghetti and meatballs.

My parents didn't smoke or drink, not even wine. My father didn't even drink coffee. He just blasted off at six a.m. on the radio running on pure adrenaline. He would wake up at five o'clock, shower, jump in his Oldsmobile and gun the engine down to Hollywood before Valley freeways were in existence. My mother would fall back to sleep before waking me up to dress and walk Ventura Boulevard to take me to school.

One day I saw a kid come to school in pajamas. Welcome to California!

My mother and I continued to spend most of every day without my father as he performed and promoted his radio program. My parents eventually grew tired of renting and wanted a larger home and property – the American Dream – so they purchased a home farther west in the San Fernando Valley.

The lot offered more land than they had been used to and afforded the construction of the Southern California mandate – a swimming pool. There were scores of swimming pool contractors available. Through old acquaintances from Connecticut – an old-world Italian couple now living nearby – my parents obtained the services of a pool builder. We were all excited, perhaps me the most.

As the pool was being filled, the builder's son stood on the top concrete step and watched as the water rose. This kid was standing in *my* pool on *my* top step watching my pool water level rise. With no consideration of the fact that he was fully clothed, I became a stealth warrior coming up behind him and, using both hands, I pushed him forward into the water.

He was soaked with extreme prejudice!

I hid under my bed until my father located me. After a less than heartfelt apology, I went underground for a few hours until dinner – barbecued burgers and salad - was served. I sincerely hope I have not led this innocent victim to a life of turmoil. I have no idea why I pushed the kid.

Yes, I do. That was *my* pool and not his.

The farther west one traveled, land was less developed. Homes were spread out with more space. There were groves of orange trees. Wide streets prevailed before the Southern California freeway system took over as the main thoroughfares. It was an octopus that allowed you to travel thousands of miles through Los Angeles County from desert to mountain to the Pacific Ocean.

My father traveled it all. He became the Willy Loman of the airwaves promoting the show, getting his name out there, having four lunches a week with strangers, gaining weight, all for hammering out an identity. My mother and I no longer walked to school or grocery stores as Ventura Boulevard wasn't around the corner from our home, or Hollywood, which was now twelve miles away, and our dentist was now in the northern part of the Valley.

My parents purchased a Volkswagen Beetle (Bug) – stick shift, twenty-five cents a gallon for gasoline, simplicity.

It would turn out to be my mother's favorite automobile.

My father's radio audience was building and he started signing off each episode with "'Bye, hon." It didn't occur to my young, inexperienced mind that there may be other "hons" listening besides my mother. My mother and father were married, had me, and would be together forever. Their relationship was a rock as far as I was concerned. Experience.

My father brought home many long-playing records that labels sent him to play on his show and promote. I discovered the power of music when I dropped the needle on the soundtrack of William Wyler's western "The Big Country."

I had no idea who Gregory Peck, Jean Simmons or Charlton Heston were or, for that matter, composer Jerome Moross. But, I knew the mighty theme music excited me. I played it over and over until my mother asked if I could play another album for her sanity.

When we went for a "ride" on Sundays, I would sing out loud from my backseat perch. I presented my version of "The Big Country" theme to my parents, testing their patience. My mother had already heard the official version dozens of times. They both loved and played all kinds of music except classical and put up with me. I stopped singing as we approached Du-

Par's in the east Valley for a hamburger.

In time, my mother's mother wore out her welcome with her oldest daughter, son-in-law and their two children back East (one older, one younger than me). My parents took the baton and flew her out West to spend time with our growing family (my mother was pregnant) and give the eastern family members a rest. My mother and grandmother soon butted heads – they had their individual modus operandi and it didn't always agree.

My grandmother enjoyed the open space of Los Angeles unlike her cramped Connecticut neighborhood where everyone knew everything about her and the family. The open space of the West also, at insecure moments, scared her. There was too much freedom of fashion – my mother wore shorts for God's sake – and lifestyle, my mother drove her own car (both my grandmothers never drove). And this impacted general opinions, there was a loose feel in the air, anyone could say or do anything at any time.

There was no tradition unlike in the East.

Citizens were making things up on the spot. Rules were being written. Roads were being paved. We were young and learning something new, daily. There was one positive aspect to Los Angeles, according to my grandmother – "The Lawrence Welk Show" was taped in town. She could relax for an hour a week. Lawrence Welk would later appear on my father's radio show and my father would drum on "The Lawrence Welk Show."

My grandmother tried to figure out how the nine pieces of the drum kit fit into the television set.

We ate dinner in shifts as my father would always arrive home late for dinner. There would be tension between my mother and grandmother left over from the day but my father could easily make my grandmother laugh and the stress would subside until tomorrow.

The West was just fine for me as I could say or sing just about anything and it would get a smile or laugh from my family and, sometimes, strangers. On an adventurous family outing to a restaurant across the road from the Pacific Ocean in Malibu, a drunk, older woman gave me five dollars because I was so adorable. I didn't have to say or sing anything for it.

My family being as Southern Californian as East Coast transplants can be, it was time for my parents to hire a gardener. One of the last white yard workers in Los Angeles, our gardener loved green lawns, newly planted shrubs, hummingbirds and bees. I think he also enjoyed chatting with my mother after she brought him a cool drink. His gasoline-powered lawn mower made quite a racket and he had every conceivable trimmer, cutter, and shovel. This was before the proverbial Southern California gardener equipment – the leaf blower – made its debut so a sturdy rake was necessary.

It was mow, rake and converse with my mother. At one point, I thought it would be fun to be his assistant, handling the tools, working the yards, riding in his truck but there was school. One day, he planted twenty junipers in our yard near the street. The next morning, as my mother backed out of the driveway to take me to school, we noticed twenty fresh holes *lacking* junipers. This was before another Southern California institution – neighborhood watch.

For myself, I couldn't have been a gardener for long anyway because I was needed back on the airwaves. My father invited me on for brief spells of song and cuteness. The response was the station manager suggesting I co-host with a trailblazing female on-air reporter a week of shows while my father was on vacation. The segments were taped over a few days – me gabbing with the reporter, reading commercial copy, introducing music and singing a few tunes. The vacation was a week at Lake Arrowhead with my father returning to Hollywood a few times to "work." My mother and I were on our own again - no Morokses though for their great hamburgers.

Back home, one day I entered the garage searching out a rake to do my own gardening. It was a windy day and there were leaves aplenty. I found the rake as a gust of wind hit the heavy wooden garage door and blew it shut. I was eight years old and didn't have the strength to push open the door. It was dark in the garage and I started to panic. I yelled out a few times but received no reaction. My mother and grandmother were inside the house and couldn't hear me. I tried the door again – minimal movement.

There was a window with four panes of glass facing the street. I yelled out again. No one heard me. I found a hammer and shattered one of the panes. After I cleared the frame of glass I wriggled through it headfirst and fell to the ground. I was free. I ran to the front door and got out of the cold air. My grandmother saw me first and screamed. Then my mother joined in. I looked around for the cause of the commotion and noticed my right hand and sleeve of my tan jacket covered in blood.

A glass chip from the windowpane had dropped on my middle finger causing the gusher. My mother and I got into the Volkswagen and headed to our doctor who closed the wound with a few stitches and told me I'd probably need a new jacket for Christmas.

My mother started to "show" her next child. Two parents, two children and a grandmother equaled a home with more rooms. $50,000 was paid for a modern home with more space and plenty of cement drive. The moving van traveled exactly one street west. I was in awe and slightly embarrassed when I heard the purchase price. I was also scared. Were my parents millionaires? No. My mother drove a Volkswagen for God's sake. The following June she gave birth to a girl whose eyes reflected my father's early years with his "Asian" look.

I was no longer solo, king of the roost. I would have to give up full attention and share life with my eight-year younger sister. My grandmother now had her own bedroom and spent all her hours with her new granddaughter.

Years later, my sister would comment that she thought her grandmother was her mother because her grandmother stood by paying attention to her every move, talking to her, and hugging her as opposed to her mother who was paying attention to a marriage breaking apart and a husband in fifth gear with no brakes.

My father began to faintly resemble my mother's boyfriend in high school. His wandering eyes would ignite heated discussions between my parents in their bedroom. I heard female names shouted that I had never heard before and didn't have a clue as to who they were. Were they co-workers at the radio station or waitresses at the Copper Skillet in Hollywood where my father would eat breakfast some mornings after he went off the air at ten o' clock?

Apparently, in the Fifties and Sixties if the gap was widening between a couple, having more children was the answer. Once I walked in my parents' bedroom unannounced. My parents were naked and something had just happened. They didn't see me and I rapidly and quietly removed myself from the room. I still feel embarrassed about seeing my unclothed mother as sex was never discussed, or naughty jokes told, or bikinis worn, or kisses given on the lips.

I had no concept of my parents making love. They were rocks of stability, not sexual beings although they also laughed and touched and kissed without shyness. But something mysterious occurred immediately before I entered the room that day, and only they knew about it. This event would never be mentioned during a car ride with my father to Hollywood or over a hamburger at Du-Par's.

Occasionally, I would study my parents and envision them together at the beginning in high school – the first time they saw each other, the first words said, and the first embrace and kiss – without in-laws and children, back when they were just kids. When did being a couple standing together against the world evolve into something more complex? They were in the same bodies but their understanding of and intentions toward each other were mutating. The rocks were losing fragments, still it was unimaginable that my parents would welcome, pay attention to, caress, or go to sleep with any *other* human being.

A couple of years later, my second sister was born after a stressful pregnancy fraught with more female names shouted out loud and the arrival of my father's brother who stayed with us for months. He was between jobs and various stays in jail. My mother paid full attention to her youngest daughter. She chose her doctor's given name as her youngest daughter's middle name. Her doctor was older, handsome, calm, and, most importantly, attentive. My sisters were eight and nine years younger than me but I still enjoyed their chubbiness and the way they crawled along the floor on their behinds.

But they were brought into the world by my parents for the wrong reasons.

My sisters were innocent. My mother loved my younger sister while my grandmother loved the middle child, my oldest younger sister. My father would spend time in the pool with all three of us. The Pool League was created where my father and I were on different teams in the major leagues playing a schedule. We used a short bat and a rubber ball. We established different zones for single, double, the deep end was a triple, for instance. Once my father hit the ball straight over the house, landing in the front yard for a home run. We kept the scores, standings and a column written by my father in a spiral notebook with a water-stained blue cover.

Occasionally, photographers would visit our home and take family photos for magazines and newspapers. My father and I smiled from the diving board at the pool. My father, sisters and I smiled atop our inflatable rafts. My father, mother, sisters and I smiled in our beautiful never used living room.

My grandmother stayed in her bedroom during family shoots. Although my father ceased the 250 personal appearance luncheons per year, he never stopped promoting his radio program. Behaving like the happy show business family for an hour or two was a faster, more efficient, mode for mass publicity. This is when media fans read the Los Angeles Times, the Herald Examiner, Photoplay and TV Guide to learn more about their favorite film, television, and radio personalities.

Showing one's face in public was still a publicist's dream. My parents and I attended the premiere of "Ben-Hur" at the Egyptian Theater on Hollywood Boulevard; my father and I attended the West Coast premiere of "Lawrence of Arabia" at the Warner Beverly Hills Theater; my parents and I were present at the opening of the Cinerama Dome in Hollywood for "It's a Mad, Mad, Mad, Mad World."

Years later my father and I walked the lush, squishy red carpet at the Pussycat Theatre on Santa Monica Boulevard for the Los Angeles premiere of "Deep Throat."

My father's sense of humor was connecting with drivers on the way to work and housewives at home starting their days getting the kids ready for school. He was becoming a household name. The station manager and sponsors were pleased. A two-hundred seat playhouse across the street from my future high school found a win-win situation with my father – he would get to be Jack Lemmon for six weeks in front of a live audience and the play ("Who Was That Lady I Saw You With?") would get free commercials every broadcast from my father. He played the lead's goofy TV writer friend who saves the lead from divorce by concocting a wild scheme.

My father literally knocked knees with the audience as he made his entrance. The sound of live laughter was drug-like, intoxicating. He was now addicted to acting, he loved it. Our family saw him even less – on the air at six in the morning, booking guests and music for his show during the day, and on-stage at night. He received good reviews and was beginning to get talked about.

But things were not always peaceful at home. My mother and grandmother would have daily confrontations on the absence of my father and how to raise children. There would be yelling, bickering, debating. My mother missed the simpler lifestyle and work hours in Connecticut. My grandmother thought my mother was ignoring her oldest daughter. Soon, my grandmother removed herself and flew back east. Her son-in-laws felt relief and pressure simultaneously. It was the cross-country hand-off, once again.

I would play with my sisters but the age difference was so severe I preferred to play army with one friend or softball with another and not Ken and Barbie dolls. When my father did make an appearance at home, everyone assaulted him, craving his attention and those precious hours with him.

There were trips to the park with my sisters, baseball in the pool with me, barbecues for birthday celebrations (family only, never friends). A night out with my mother at the Cocoanut Grove/Ambassador Hotel to see Harry Belafonte, a drive around Valley neighborhoods to look at homes on the market when my parents were perfectly content with their present residence, but enjoyed window shopping.

My father's parents missed their youngest son and grew tired of Connecticut winters so they sold their home and drove west. They found an unassuming home in a new Valley development twenty minutes from us. My grandfather continued working in furniture sales while my grandmother cleaned and prepared dinner every day. At six pm, my grandfather had a pour of bourbon, a cigarette and a Lawrence Welk record on the turntable. Occasionally, our family visited my grandparents on Sundays where they would bicker over the most trivial matter and my grandfather told mind-numbing, long-winded stories about relatives or the latest from the furniture store. He would catch me day-dreaming and pull me into his tale by proclaiming, "You're in this!" My mother would break into laughter.

I was in the fourth grade at a public elementary school during this time. Each year was split into two semesters – B and A. I was one of the best and brightest in my class and the A portion of the year was basically just review. Therefore, my teacher wanted to promote me to the fifth grade –B5 – and skip A4. I enjoyed school but I relished my friends – one friend I played shortstop to his second base in a school softball league and the other friend I played army with because his family had a great backyard complete with a creek. And, besides, the girl I was in love with (I suggested her name for my youngest sister, my parents liked it) was in my class. She was a lot smarter than I was. She was Jewish, I was Catholic, quickly losing interest in religion every Sunday as I listened to a cold mass spoken in Latin and thought about the pro football games I was missing.

There was no celebration at home, no "way to go!" No cake, no hamburger at Du- Par's, no input from my parents. My parents behaved in their small-town, eastern way: do your work - don't get too excited about anything. I didn't. I stayed with my friends – I still know one (the second baseman who is the funniest person I've ever known – self-deprecating, obtuse observations, no boundaries). The intelligent girl and I never became boyfriend and girlfriend. She would become a cheerleader in high school then much later, a district judge in adulthood.

I remember an 8mm home movie epic, "I Was a Teenager for the FBI," which was written and directed by my father, starring my father, mother, sisters, grandparents, aunt and cousins, filmed at our home, Hollywood, the Valley, and my father's radio station. I was the FBI agent (all of twelve), my female cousin as my secretary, and male cousin as a hostage of the bad guy played by my father with glee. A Coming Attractions package was added at the end with, most memorably, "Get Me Out of This House!" starring my mother.

Occasionally, during muted arguments between my parents in their bedroom, I heard a woman's name mentioned repeatedly. Somehow, I learned the woman was a singer on a popular television variety series. She had reddish hair similar to my mother's reddish, blonde hair. I also overheard my father's secretary's name referred to, followed by denials from my father.

My father came alive when he was trying to be funny. He knew he wasn't the smartest or brightest mind in the room but he was the quickest and the sharpest. His timing took one off-guard all with a straight face. His radio show kept growing in listener numbers and he secured small roles in television shows and movies.

Producers knew that hiring him would mean free advertising on his morning show. He played the kooky neighbor semi-regularly on a corny comedy series that my oldest sister and I poked fun at relentlessly. We – five and thirteen years old – had no idea how hard it was to be an actor trying to get roles, learn dialogue, and film all day while doing a daily radio show in the morning. To us he was just our father. He could do anything we thought. We had no experience to give us insight into what his challenges might be.

My parents had seen Frank Sinatra and big bands at theaters in New York City. The new wave of sound was here and my father, mother, her sister, and I attended the very first Beatles concert in Los Angeles at the Hollywood Bowl. None of us could hear the music above the jet engine roar of the mainly young, female audience. The experience gave my father a lot to talk about on his next radio show – big bands versus the English Invasion of long-haired pop/rock artists and what it all meant.

Family outings to Du-Par's for a hamburger were infrequent as my father was no longer just a radio voice but now a television face. In between bites of his cheeseburger, a television watcher would approach our table and ask for an autograph. Most of the time paper and pen had to be found. My father never said no, much to the exasperation of my oldest sister and me, and always had a smile on his face.

Our youngest sister only saw stars around my father's face as she idolized him. My mother said nothing and my grandmother tried to figure out who these strangers were and what they wanted from our innocent family.

A long-shot break was earned by my father – an opportunity to star in a network comedy series about World War Two only twenty years after the genuine World War Two had ended. My father's acting heroes, Jack Lemmon and Gig Young, did comedy and drama roles, why not emulate them? The black and white pilot sold, and the series went into full-color production that summer.

The network and sponsors loved what they were seeing and the feeling on the set among performers, directors and producers was that the program was going to be popular. My father reluctantly retired from his radio series and said "Bye, hon" for the last time to become a full- time television mug.

The ten-to-twelve hour filming days were worse than radio days. We saw our father on weekends unless he traveled out of town to promote the new series. Sometimes, my mother traveled with him to New York so she could squeeze in a visit with her sister and family in the east. My grandmother watched my sisters while I pretended I was the man of the house.

One night my grandmother woke me up to announce that there was someone on the roof. I nervously dialed the police, with my grandmother huddled nearby, while I questioned out loud why the burglar wouldn't try a window or a door?

I would see my father for long spells during the summer when I rode with him to work (I read other roles aloud while he practiced his dialogue), spent the whole day watching filming (I learned each crew member's function and stood in line with men in uniform waiting for our steak and potato lunch), and rode home with him. My sisters had their time with him on weekends at the public park. When the series became popular, there was still no celebration at our home except for a holiday party with cast and crew.

My father was a long way from being a jewelry salesman in Stamford, Connecticut by then.

One of the last visits to my father's radio station involved entering the building through a back door that led to Columbia Records recording studio. There were five long-haired, young lads trying to enter the building. My father announced that he had a key. I looked at each face. I was in shock. He opened the door and the longhairs entered. Later, I said to my father, "Do you know who those guys were?" My father shook his head "no." "The Byrds!" I said, my excitement still palpable. It didn't mean a thing to him. They weren't Count Basie or Louie Belson or Glenn Miller.

The World War Two comedy series debuted and was an instant hit with millions of viewers and Madison Avenue advertising companies. Some of the Jewish cast members had escaped the Nazis just over twenty years ago. One of the cast members shared his numbered tattoo on his left forearm from a Nazi concentration camp where the rest of his family had all died. The war was still a painful reality to many people, but now they might be able to laugh.

I looked forward to summers spent with my father during his filming days and nights in Hollywood and Culver City where I sneaked onto sets involving Andy Griffith, Gomer Pyle and "I Spy." I came face to face with a make-up-less "That Girl." Otherwise, my father was a kind of Uncle Daddy to my sisters and mother. He had rolled the dice leaving his radio days behind him, and it had paid off.

At the end of the first wildly successful television season, the only female regular cast member mysteriously departed the program. Years later, I would hear through the grapevine that the actress and my father had had an affair and her husband gave her an ultimatum – the show or their marriage. She chose her husband. Another actress was cast. This actress read the daily call sheet – detailing scenes to be filmed and cast members involved – and started a slow, relentless climb to secure number one on the list. Number one of course was my father.

Although only fifteen miles separated my parents on any given day, they were in two distinct worlds. There was the world of New York television executives, guest actresses, Playboy Bunnies paying visits to the set to see my father and other cast members. Then there was the world of the gardener, the plumber, the electrician paying visits to see my mother who was in charge of keeping the modern home, with plenty of gleaming cement drive, running.

The arguments between my mother and grandmother continued – my grandmother claiming that my mother was not paying enough attention to my oldest sister. My father would spend weekends out of town promoting the television series with appearances on programs such as the one hosted by his hero Arthur Godfrey or as grand marshal of parades or hand-shaking his way through the rosters of local television stations.

Occasionally, my mother would join him but most of the time my father flew solo or so my mother thought. My parents' foundation had been unstable for years – the birth of my sisters only added to my mother's lockdown at home.

My father basically behaved like a single man unless he was at home trying to lighten the tension with my mother, being a weekend dad with my sisters, or tolerating my grandmother. A new, unpredictable, chaotic week began on Monday when I would resume my self-appointed role as little man of the house.

My oldest sister and I didn't make fun of the World War Two series that recognized our father as the number one player on the daily call sheet. I loved the program as I loved "Combat!," "The Great Escape," and "Von Ryan's Express." WW2 was still the razor's edge of historical reference points but, of course, in a few years the Korean War, and then Vietnam would receive most of the viewers' attention.

Life at home reflected no grand change in accoutrement. My mother infrequently dusted off her fur coat, teased her coif, and applied make-up for a trip with my father to the Hollywood Palladium for a televised awards spectacle. My sisters and I would watch to see if we could identify our mother in the crowd. My grandmother had always been a fan of radio. I think she missed my father's radio program more than my mother did.

We lived in a Valley burg that TV Guide described as "unfashionable," my sisters and I attended public schools, my parents drove American cars, we ate canned vegetables, and our barbecues rarely accepted non-family members. Much of my father's "back room" at our house which supported a set of drums, vinyl records, audio recording equipment, a hi-fi, microphones, and speakers, was soon transferred to his dressing room at the studio.

During the long stretches of downtime where sets were relit and camera angles changed, my father would drum to loud jazz. Executives, actors and actresses, musicians, and salespersons visited the stage for recognition, self-promotion, or to sell products such as video recording machines, face cream and cake flour.

Number five or six on the call sheet had an acquaintance that was marketing video units all over Hollywood. My father bit and our family became the first on our block to be able to video record birthday parties, graduations, and the kids doing cannonballs in the pool and instantly replay the results on a monitor. My father recorded two of my school friends and I desperately trying to emulate our latest musical favorites Cream. His facial expression reflected our lack of musical experience.

Although my father was now a full-fledged television entity, he had no personal assistants, no drivers, and he still did his banking in person during lunch in full costume. My mother had no maids, no support at home aside from my grandmother. The small-town thinking of the east had traveled west to the dowdy Valley hub.

An Emmy Award nomination plaque or an enlarged photograph of a film or television appearance got hammered onto the faux-bamboo wallpapered back room wall every so often but that room, supporting aural and visual communication, was on its own orbit in relation to the rest of the home.

My mother almost never entered that space except when she caught me examining my father's abundant collection of Playboy magazines. My face turned as red as her reddish-blonde hair. I told her I thought I might be interested in writing for a living. My mother savored this bust for when my father got home and she could tell him. The stack of Playboys was nothing compared to what he was perpetuating during his down time.

Some of my male friends got the "sex talk" from their fathers on a walk around the neighborhood or in the car on the way to the hardware store. My father's "birds and bees talk" took place in his dressing room that was turned into my personal theater for a sixteen-millimeter presentation of a starring turn by a performer named Candy Barr.

I never once thought about having popcorn.

I didn't know any girls (women) who emulated Ms. Barr. Junior high had been fun because of the roster of upper scale kids who arrived in Jaguars and Mercedes and had experienced more (travel, restaurants, sex) than my friends who lived in the flats west of their hilltop homes.

The hilltop girls were sexier and faster I heard. They had reputations as great kissers and sexually advanced performers. I was still trying to figure out (imagine) how pieces fit and how to unlock the gate that girls had control of. Why would a girl want to kiss me let alone perform like Ms. Barr? I wandered through a make out party once trying to ascertain how two people began the act of kissing. Did it have to involve love? Or was "like" good enough? It all returned to the magical "experience" that my father had alluded to.

I wondered, were my parents involved at the love or like level after three children and years of marriage?

Inspired by my father's love of photography, which my mother happened upon (was it the redhead singer on television?) during a rare foray into my father's space – the back room – I took a photography class in high school.

A girl (two years younger than me from a divorced family I learned) and I seized a moment between developing film and fixing images in the darkroom and started making out. She had soft, full, pillow-like lips. The moment had nothing to do with like or love. It had to do with lust – no plan, just an opportunity presented and acted upon by two young people waiting for images to appear.

Older people seemed on the surface to have no fear of closeness, a willingness to unlock the gate, no negotiation. I watched my father film scenes with the new actress where they kissed. When the camera stopped rolling, they still touched, looked into each other's eyes, smiled or laughed, and whispered things.

Was this closeness part of the actor's technique to be real? It was a television comedy for God's sake not a foreign film – commercialism versus art. How could my father share himself with one woman during the day and another woman at night? Was his ego that large? Was his paying attention method acting? Was he in love with her? Or only in lust?

My mother was spending more and more time with doctors – an ache here, an ailment there. Attention. Professional, wise, smart, caring males for the most part but doctors in general making my mother feel important, the only person that mattered, how my father made the new cast member feel, an effective bedside manner.

My parents were in separate orbits.

My father felt loved by the viewing public and the new actress, while pulling down a solid paycheck, his dream of performing having become a reality. By contrast, my mother felt trapped with three children, her mother, and a modern home, taking care of the daily mundane routine of keeping the American Dream alive, but, for whom?

My father was never home. My mother's doctors always seemed available. Get me out of this house. Kids at school who knew my father was an actor but never had reason to speak with me now suddenly approached. "I heard about your parents" - words from home from their parents who hated or loved the television series.

My mother and father were the first on our block to get divorced. Another show business casualty so far removed from the parents who were attorneys, doctors and salespeople. My sisters and I were embarrassed that our family's dirty laundry was being exposed to friends and families we knew and didn't know.

My parents' divorce represented a massive shift from sweethearts to adults.

They had seemed like kids racing each other home from CBS Television City after a taping of "The Smothers Brothers Comedy Hour" where my father appeared with Bette Davis and the Buffalo Springfield band.

Which American automobile would pull onto the cement drive first at our home in the unfashionable suburb? Did it matter who arrived first? Was this competition a game, a sexual spark left over from their early years together? Follow the leader, more crazy friends than lovers, trying to recapture the abandon of their youth before there were goals and careers and homes and children?

I would ride with my mother watching her speed along Hollywood streets through Laurel Canyon onto Ventura Boulevard to the West Valley. Although my father had the advantage of driving like a mad person every morning, my mother on occasion would pull onto the drive first. Did my father let her "win" or was he distracted by something else? When they met up at home there was a laughter release, then calm as my mother attended to the children and my father disappeared into the back room.

One year, my father was in Chicago performing a play. I was at home pacing, listening, and watching my mother having an animated phone conversation with him. There was a female voice in the background in my father's hotel room. It was the female cast member of the television series. My mother had been paying bills and discovered a foreign signature on many of the gasoline receipts. My father came clean and my mother responded with screaming and crying.

She felt betrayed.

The phone conversation went on too long, going over the same territory with the female voice in the background telling my mother to back off, step aside, the relationship was over. My mother slammed the phone into the receiver easily a dozen times shrieking and weeping. My sisters and I exchanged looks of uncertainty while my grandmother tried to console her daughter to no avail.

My parents' twenty-year marriage lay in ruins.

When my father returned to Los Angeles, he cleared away his clothing and electronic equipment while his children were at school. My mother was grieving day and night as my grandmother tiptoed through the house cleaning, cooking, and taking care of her granddaughters. The rock that was my parents union had rolled over the edge of a cliff and lay shattered in a million pieces.

The kings and queens of the show business world of gossip said my father was cheating with an actress and my mother was cheating with her physician. I hid for the rest of the school year. My sanctuary was my photography friend from a divorced family. I would spend time at her home kissing her and playing Creedence Clearwater Revival records. I felt as if I were in a different town though I was fifteen minutes from home.

I never looked at my parents the same from those days forward. Trust was terminated. I was acquiring experience of the worst kind, blaming our family for not being interesting enough to hold my *father's* attention.

Our home was set directly on a fault line that no one paid heed. There had been tremors over the years and now the big one finally hit. My friends didn't know what to say to me although they did make me laugh. In time I graduated high school. My mother attended. My father was out of town working making money to pay for two households.

I never witnessed physical violence between my parents. They didn't drink or take drugs. Their most uncomfortable conversations involved strange female names being mentioned. Except for the phone call we heard and observed and my father's empty closets and workroom the sun still shone, the television played and we dove in our beautiful pool. The slowly moving colossal wave had crashed, done irreparable damage and then retreated.

My mother was now a single parent. My father lived somewhere else. I saw him more than he saw my sisters because I could drive to him to visit his new world where a woman other than my mother held his hand, whispered in his ear and slept in the same bed. She smoked and drank wine, unlike my mother. She owned income property, something that my parents could have invested in for a rainy day. She seemed smarter than my mother but my mother was sweeter and kinder. My mother was five years older than her, as well, which in its own way became another cliche.

Four months after my parents divorced, my father and his woman friend, the only regular female name on the television series' call sheet, his confidant and lover and carrier of their baby, exchanged wedding vows on the stage where they filmed.

I thought it was tacky for them to get married there.

My father's parents attended, my sisters and I did not because we felt sadness and anger emanating from my mother, and our loyalty lay with her. The new wife had told my mother to step aside and she reluctantly did. New mama was solidifying her position by amalgamating with a television personality watched and adored by millions of viewers, thus providing more comfortable quarters for her daughter from a previous marriage.

The Anchor Baby was the meal ticket in the wings.

In the Seventies, the scandal of having a baby out of wedlock could terminate a career, thus, a marriage ceremony was the only card in the deck that trumped all the other scenarios. With the union and the baby, the power grid belonged to my new stepmother. My father had paved the road and controlled the speed and direction of his relationship with my mother. Now, he turned the driver's wheel over to his seven-year younger spouse. He would earn the salary, and she would pull the business strings. She had bought and sold homes and income properties. My parents had owned part of an orange grove in the San Joaquin Valley in California, it was money losing, the best venture they could do.

My sisters perceived our new stepmother as the cause of our parents' break-up. It was more complicated than that. My father was exposed to new creative people every day and experienced work and play episodes in new cities almost every week. My mother was at home exposed to children, her mother, and the same home maintenance routine she experienced every day. Now there was a new sexually charged mate who was willing to leave her daughter with a sitter while she traveled the world on a first-class basis.

Nothing and no one would get in *her* way.

My parents had spent twenty-plus years together from the innocence of high school love, through the de rigueur wedding to escaping small-town trappings to becoming pioneers and traveling west across the country. I'm convinced that children got in the way of any advancement for them as a couple. The wanderlust for my parents as a couple ceased as they bought a home and settled into society's expectations. Wild abandon was discontinued.

'Get me out of this house' was originated.

The modern home still belonged to my mother but it was now a dead set for my father. He had done his thing here – provided laughter, played drums, jumped in the pool (always feet first) – but, more importantly, taken the first steps toward adulthood. One couldn't be an adult living side-by-side with one's high school sweetheart. My father's drive and daily experiences wouldn't allow it.

There was no looking back for my father. He developed the beginnings of a shell that safeguarded him against memory. The hardness of my stepmother also changed him. The first few years were challenging for my sisters and me as we watched our father attempt to satisfy his new mate. She was a woman who possessed a core that soon demonstrated a lack of natural kindness or sweetness that my mother possessed in her blood.

My stepmother was a lone lioness who only traveled in packs with *males*. She had no room for stepdaughters, mothers-in-law, let alone an ex-wife. Her own daughter retreated to her room more and more after getting a sense of how the future would play out – a new man and his family taking more time away from a daughter trying to be noticed by her ever-distancing, emotionally cold mother.

My half-brother was born complete with my *father's* and *my* first name. The name was the first name of my stepmother's favorite stepfather, she claimed. I looked around for backup. Did anyone else hear this, my father, for instance? Eventually, my father, feeling a bit awkward, told me not to worry, that my half-brother would be called by his middle name and *not* his first.

Castration. Power. A new era complete with collateral damage.

The time of the multi-part Christmas Eve began. I would drive my sisters over to our father and stepmother's home for a meal and opening presents. There was always a modicum of tension in the air based on what sort of day our stepmother had experienced.

Most of her day was the seeming dread of her stepchildren arriving and redirecting our father's attention away from her for a few hours. Our stepsister told private jokes to herself, our stepmother lit cigarette after cigarette, and poured another glass of red wine and our father played his best pretend light comedy Jack Lemmon, a little befuddled, a little ignorant of the distress in the room, playing dumb.

I never knew what to gift my father. As a teenager, I walked to the drug store and bought after-shave lotion for him. When we began New Christmas at his new abode, I delivered a large, awkward mass-produced print of a father and small son walking hand in hand. It was corny. In the end, it never found wall space at their home.

During one memorable Christmas Eve get together, in an air of détente, our stepsister offered some powder-covered sweets to my sisters. My oldest sister took a bite as our stepsister broke into uncontrollable laughter. She signaled to her mother who almost gagged on her wine. There was an hysterical roar between this mother and daughter duo. My sister carefully examined the sweet. She brushed the powder away.

It was a piece of dog excrement covered in powdered sugar.

On the verge of tears, my sister couldn't believe it. There was madness in the air. My father attended to my sister and stared at his wife and stepdaughter, uncomprehending, which only produced more jeering, as he looked at his new wife as if he didn't know her.

There comes a time in every relationship when one thinks about jumping ship theoretically or actually. The candy/dog shit gag previewed what was coming for my sisters and me. Although our father had left our mother, we wanted happiness for him. We tried to visit with him on our own as much as possible but even *that* evolved into the twenty dollar bill drop off in Westwood for my sisters and riding in his car as he did errands for me.

I was still in awe of my father who had attained major success in television and radio and who supported two households now. He was a man. He was experienced. I was young and searching. How or why could I tell my father how to live his life? "Don't make waves" was his motto, and I tried to emulate that. As my sisters and I now shared his hours in the minority, we all hoped for steady seas during times like Christmas Eve and other holidays.

We wished him the best but as one takes a bite of dog shit and sees one's new 'mother' howling with glee, and her damaged daughter bent over with laughter, it's hard to wish anything but failure for this kind of twisted relationship. Our mother never – couldn't – create such ugly scenarios, but the stepmother delighted in doing just that.

Was this new parental figure, diabolical, scheming, and unhappy with everyone else in the room except herself? Was our father her mirror somehow – the former altar boy gone bad – or was he just plain weak?

Our grandmother – our father's mother – sealed her fate as she clipped her fingernails at the dining table. Was this action somehow a spike back at her daughter-in-law or small town, high school dropout sensibilities in motion? As distressing as her deed was, when she did that, I howled inside, cheering on the insanity of this circus show.

My mother, who had never held a job, decided to volunteer at a local hospital. She greeted patients and visited rooms to make sure the inhabitants were comfortable. She began a brief affair with an Italian-American man upon his release from the hospital, who had family in Italy. Soon, it was our grandmother holding down the fort as our mother took off for Italy for a week to meet la familia.

The relationship didn't work ultimately so her longtime friend from Connecticut – the only female friend in Los Angeles for a spell – invited her on a Mexican cruise. Grandmother in place, our mother took off again. ABC Television was having a promotion for their fall series onboard and "Dan August," the star

Burt Reynolds, took a shine to this older blonde. Back on terra firma, a couple of dates occurred – Burt displaying his charm, our mother displaying her quietude, but nothing came of it as our mother didn't know how to play Hollywood.

She wasn't provocative nor a sex kitten nor a performer but a divorced hausfrau from an unfashionable Valley burg. Later, Reynolds would move onto a much older blonde Dinah Shore.

There was a problem with the dating game – my mother still loved my father.

After six seasons, my father's series was canceled. He hit the road again playing cities in the Midwest and south. His new wife traveled with him occasionally but because they had a toddler she spent more time at home which afforded my father opportunities to meet and greet bar maidens, store clerks, front desk attendants, et. al.

There was too much free time on the dinner theater circuit. The temptation to sleep with a television personality permeated many meetings he had with the local workforce and fans. Husbands and boyfriends were jettisoned for the chance to encounter a representative of Hollywood. Film was exposed and videotape was rolling in every city he performed in, the documents became a sociological thesis on women's sexual behavior and hairstyles across the United States it seemed.

My father's ego was in a tailspin as he was no longer appearing on weekly network television. He produced his own pictures and shared the photo albums of nude women from Lake Charles, Louisiana, Cincinnati, Ohio, and Traverse City, Michigan, with anyone who would look at them.

There were no censors in his thought process and decision-making. After one turn as the star of a movie, Disney executives had had enough of my father when "set spies" reported that he was offering crew members a look at his Polaroid collection of topless waitresses, strippers and actresses.

Walt must have turned over in his grave.

My stepmother realized that her number one on the call sheet was out of control but he was making money on the road and sending it home to pay for the mock Tudor spread in the hills of Westwood. If there were a divorce this time around it would cost plenty. My stepmother had the mind and skills of a cold, heartless Century City attorney.

My college girlfriend and I were in our early twenties, our main skills being new movie watchers and pizza connoisseurs around town. She was an artist and I was a wannabe movie maker. Time to get married! Her parents and my father and stepmother gave us the thumbs up. Her parents must have considered financial backup on my side, while my stepmother tried to erase as many family members on her husband's side as possible.

My mother nixed the proposition. She saw another relationship derailment up ahead. This decision mirrored her feelings about all women I would be with in the future: no woman would ever be accepted - arms wide open - in the coming decades including two wives, I married and loved.

My father was now under the spell of his latest wife – she watched the bank account, making a property investment from time to time, allowing him his indiscretions on the road, with seeming indifference. She was kind of a cool mother figure, letting you "get away with it" if you studied – and I could tell he felt some residual pain and regret for his former high school sweetheart, my mother, that he had left behind.

My father proposed that my mother sell their old modern home and begin anew in the hills of the unfashionable suburb. He would help her with the purchase. They met at the realtor's office and exchanged introductions with the agent, a man around my father's age, shorter, a smoker, fast on his feet with numbers, plain looking but possessing a killer smile. They all looked at a few model homes but nothing came of it.

I stood with my father watching his latest home video that he had edited, a compilation of the best moments of The Tonight Show starring Johnny Carson. We were in the basement, the latest backroom when a thunderous commotion emanated from the stairway. My oldest sister lay in a crumpled ball at the foot of the stairs. My father yelled out his wife's name, again and again, but she did not respond. Did she not hear him?

My sister would have bruises but, fortunately, nothing was broken or shattered; still, no stepmother. My sister announced that as she descended the steep stairway she was pushed from behind. Our father ascended the stairs to find his wife sitting in the kitchen nook at the circular table overlooking the university while she calmly sipped a glass of red wine and took a drag off yet another Marlboro cigarette. He yelled where had she been during this near disaster? In a detached cadence she proclaimed that she had *not* heard his cries.

When an actor or actress is known primarily for one role it's a blessing that one experienced success and a curse that one's talents are handcuffed to one character. My father played bad guys in television series guest star roles and conjured tears in another but he was still his greatest success – a little older and thicker – but with the same eyes and sense that he was about to smoothly deliver a punchline.

The country's dinner theater circuit paid well but the salary was supporting two homes and families and an occasionally bad or underperforming investment on my stepmother's part. My father received a two hundred dollar allowance check at the beginning of the month by his accountant. That was all he ever used.

My mother was gardening in her yard as the real estate agent drove by at the end of his day nearly screeching to a halt as he made note of her striped Capri pants. He turned around and pulled into the cement drive. A two-hour conversation began, touching upon new homes, his Jaguar, home life and relationships. He was married – twenty years, no children. They had just drifted apart. He wanted peace and stability and she wanted a larger home. Divorce was in his future. My mother announced she didn't date married men. They went to dinner the next evening, anyway.

I would spend time with my father, which meant driving the streets of Los Angeles on the eternal errand run: picking up dry cleaning, grocery shopping, dropping off film to be developed, picking up a power cord or a converter adapter for a videotape deck or a monitor.

My father threw out amusing comments to grocery cashiers,

gas station attendants, and the employee taking orders at the fast food stand. He wrote on his feet, with nothing drafted on paper. He adlibbed nine years of a radio show on Los Angeles airwaves but never wrote anything down. He would never have the patience to sit down and put ideas and dialogue together for a script. My father was not Alan Alda – actor, writer, director of television and films. He directed his perennial comedy play, which was almost like delivering a stand-up routine every single night.

A laugh from a crewmember on a television episode being filmed was not enough. He wanted laughter now. He returned to radio recording programs for Armed Forces Radio and specials for his former rival station in Los Angeles. The engineer's control booth was packed with station employees and advertising executives. He didn't hear the laughter emanating from the other side of the glass partition but he saw the facial expressions connoting amusement. My father was back creating improvised routines and gags off the top of his head – nothing to write, nothing to memorize, everything instantaneous, gratification in the moment. He was quick, spontaneous, and there was no one like him.

I sat in the passenger seat and studied my father's handsome face. His countenance was perfect for the television screen – a wide, infectious grin, sharing a secret with the audience. Radio wasted his looks while movies seldom asked for any expression from the leading man.

I had broken up with my college girlfriend – we "loved" each other but there were too many other distractions namely men and women – my draft number (55) had been called months

My UnHollywood Family

My UnHollywood Family

My UnHollywood Family

BOB CRANE:
Is this the next addition to the Family Affair?

Looks like it just might be. With Bob's background as a disc jockey, he has much experience and know-how to pass on to his son's new group, the "Jug Band." Not only do they have this but Bob is also a recording enthusiast and has all the equipment necessary to set them up for a professional session. With this kind of backing who can miss. Naturally, Bob Jr. is the drummer—naturally because Bob Sr. (now the star of the successful CBS series *Hogan's Heroes*) was once a professional drummer. In photo, right, you can see Bob on the drummer at a recent recording session and you'll note that even music doesn't take him far from the set of *Hogan's Heroes*.

Bob adjusts and sets up his recording equipment for the "Jug Band."

Bob holds the mike for better balance as the boys prepare to record their "hit."

The boys, Ronnie Heck, Bob Jr. and Dave Arnoff are joined by Bob on the tambourine.

Even Bob's wife, Anne, joins the family affair every chance she gets.

The girls, Karen 6, and Debbie, 7 practice so they can join the group.

36 APRIL 1967

54

My UnHollywood Family

55

ago and I skated a trip to Vietnam – and my college days were numbered – I disliked having to spend hours in Geology and Science classes all in the name of a Bachelor of Arts degree. One didn't need a B.A. to oversee a craft service table or to be a stand-in on a movie set. I had performed that function at my father's previous Disney gig many times over.

There was one last item to take care of for a film class: co-write with my best friend a paper on our fresh acting discovery, Jack Nicholson.

We finagled an interview with the new Brando at his home sharing a driveway with the original Brando. We talked film for hours and received an A for our efforts. But we were just starting. We ate up "Easy Rider," "Five Easy Pieces" and "Carnal Knowledge." We interviewed his co-actors, directors and writers. Three years later we had a book. My ex-college girlfriend's father who wrote television episodes helped us secure an agent. We had a book deal!

I asked my father if we could hold a book launch party at his home. I was excited that all our writing, research and travel paid off with the *first* book about Nicholson. He looked at me and wanted to know why we would do that because he never did that. The book launch sank instantly. Nevertheless, Nicholson expressed satisfaction with the finished product, although he spotted an identification miscue within seconds of cracking open the tome.

I often wondered why my mother and father never celebrated work, birthdays, marriage…life. My mother was always looking into the past and my father was always looking into the future. They were never in the present.

The past stops you in your tracks. The future drives you toward someone or something you think you must have, like the star stripper at the Classic Cat on Sunset Boulevard. For my father's birthday my stepmother thought her husband should celebrate – with a tete-a-tete with the headliner. My father disappeared backstage while my stepmother sipped her ever present glass of red wine and mentally moved another chess piece in her head.

One memorable day, my stepmother's daughter fainted in her room. My father drove her to the ER at the University Hospital where the physician announced that she had "overdosed" on marijuana. My father was livid. Contrary to the physician, my stepsister kept repeating that she hadn't smoked pot.

Back at home, my oldest sister overheard our stepmother tell her daughter to never tell her stepfather that she smokes pot all the time. My sister reported what she'd heard to our father, who later told our stepmother that my sister had told him what she had overheard. Our stepmother called my sister a liar and announced that she didn't want my sister in the house after that. Our stepsister told my oldest sister that her mother had in fact given her the money to buy the pot. My stepmother also regularly shared wine and other alcohol with her daughter who was underage at the time.

Once, at a restaurant while my father was in the restroom, my oldest sister witnessed something strange. She told our father that his wife shared his Screwdriver with her daughter to drink from. When our father returned to the table, my sister started crying because the stepmother and her daughter had both consumed some of his drink and he didn't know it.

Our father confronted his wife later in the evening with my stepmother retorting that his daughter was a "spoiled crybaby" who wanted to ruin a big family get-together. We were all called liars at one time or another with my young namesake being his mother's latest disciple.

There were constant accusations like my youngest sister "broke" our half-brother's arm. She was, in fact, "watching" him when he fell from a swing in the backyard, but my stepmother couldn't accept that it was an accident that resulted in his broken arm.

There were jealousies. My stepmother wanted my father all for herself – no sharing him with his daughters, his mother, or his ex-wife. She put up with me for a while because I exhibited no force or command to defy her. She named her son, giving him my first name, in a power play. I was a lackey in my father's army.

The woman from Bakersfield who had *four* stepfathers exhibited ice water veins and a complete disrespect and contempt for the powerless.

The realtor was spending consecutive nights at the old modern home. My oldest sister walked into my mother's bedroom and witnessed them in flagrante delicto. The scene had a greater impact on my sister than my seeing my mother nude when I was a youngster. There was a man other than our father in bed with our mother, and it must have felt horribly wrong to her.

Men's clothing took over my father's former closet and a shiny maroon Jaguar found its place on the cement drive one afternoon. One afternoon, my parents were having a monetary discussion on the telephone when the subject turned to my stepmother's rage over her son's arm having been "broken" by my youngest sister. My stepmother wanted my sister to appear before a tribunal consisting of my stepmother as judge and jury.

My father wanted to avoid his marriage imploding. My mother handed the telephone to her man to speak some sense with her ex-man. The new boyfriend listened as my father pleaded his case. Please could he pick up my youngest sister and deliver her to his wife's courtroom, anything to keep the peace, his voice seemed to say. Nothing more was said as the boyfriend juggled and processed the appeal in his mind. Then with stark clarity he told my father that if this "alleged crime" was that important to my father's marriage, then he doesn't have a marriage.

My father deflated on the other end of the telephone. He agreed with his ex-wife's boyfriend. No trial. No gulag. My mother was impressed with her boyfriend's forthrightness and bravery speaking directly as to the right thing to do with her celebrity ex-husband. Of course, the next time my youngest sister visited our father at his home he marched her upstairs to his bedroom and made his daughter apologize to her stepmother.

My father could sell the product he knew best: himself. Marketing himself was another matter that involved attending and/or hosting parties, appearing at awards shows, and taking small roles in films or television programs that demonstrated skills previously unseen by producers, directors, and studio executives.

Although he missed the World War Two TV series it was time to display new chords like his hero Jack Lemmon – drama, comedy, comedy, drama. Our Willy Loman was tired of being on the road. He wanted to copulate in his own bed for a change. The best his talent agent could come up with was a tired, third-tier situation comedy produced for one of the most successful television series providers in the entertainment industry at that time.

Mary Tyler Moore's company was a perennial winner until this series that took a year-and-a-half to produce thirteen half-hour episodes. From a one-camera with no audience pilot to a three-camera with audience series couldn't haul the shopworn scripts out of the mud.

My father was home earning a paycheck but was very unhappy. He missed the wildness of live radio and the fun of outsmarting Nazis. The new series was thankfully euthanized after thirteen forgettable episodes. Nowadays, the cans of film may never have been taken off the shelf. My father grabbed at the next chance to hit the road knowing that his tried-and-true hour-and-a-half comedy play with four characters would generate live laughter every night.

Movable video was the rage and it became one of the entertainment stops for my father's on-the-road playgroup. Some cast members imbibed in alcoholic beverages or marijuana; others displayed their bodies for the camera lens; some took it a leap forward and enacted their behind the bedroom door proclivities all for the sake of instant enjoyment. Often, non-pros would join the ensemble. The clunky camera resembled something from Uzbekistan television in the Fifties, but everybody was a star when in front of the camera's gaze.

The half-inch videotape was reel-to-reel. The recording machine in a steel carrying case appeared like an amplifier for a rock band. My father's stage directorial skills carried over into a hotel room or an apartment cubicle. The players never got enough. They laughed, yelled, criticized and came back for more. My father never asked his representative about a job directing a television episode. He was directing every day on the road on-stage and off. Although he participated on-camera, his thrill was the act of capturing behavioral abandon on tape by willing performers.

My father should have been a documentarian for the liberated narcissist.

In time, the realtor married my mother and became an instant parent to three children. I gradually trusted him as he showed a simple, hard work ethic that he developed on his own with no help from his parents. He had no siblings and no children from his first marriage. He showed me that he clearly loved and adored my mother by standing up to my father.

My stepfather was the new protector. He was an Air Force veteran, had no use for the film and television industries, enjoyed baseball, and followed a low-key approach to getting what he wanted as a commercial and residential landlord.

I learned how to conduct conversations with people one knew nothing about or couldn't have cared less about hearing of their past or present lives. I observed how my stepfather extrapolated information from perfect strangers with ease. I liked him. It was tough, though, to tell my father that my new stepfather was a good guy. My oldest sister rode the fence on the new marriage and my youngest sister would never be swayed by anyone other than her blood paternal figure.

After my father's latest television series departed, I took it upon myself to help him with publicity. We had done the father and son standing on the pool diving board photograph and the father-son-daughters riding bicycles photograph and the father-mother-son-daughters arriving at the premiere photograph.

Now, it was time to get some answers as in a Q & A session. I would disguise my name so the piece would have some credibility. I chose my middle name and my stepfather's last name. Cassette player rolling tape, I interviewed my father in his latest back room. Barbara Walters had nothing to fear but my questions did push my father to concentrate and construct thought-out answers with occasional touches of humor.

I transcribed the interview and sent it to a randomly chosen editor at Playboy-owned *Oui Magazine* that I admired for the writers, interviews and, yes, the international models. The editor liked the interview but I had to come clean about my true identity and my relationship to the subject.

The question and answer pages were tossed but I pitched an interview with Bruce Dern and got an assignment. Then I had to explain the rejection to my father whose only comment was "Who's Bruce Dern?" I was a step closer to that stack of Playboy Magazines in the closet of my father's original back room at the old house; I was a step closer to becoming a writer.

I was eight and nine years older than my sisters who were still trying to figure out why our parents were not together. Their friends blamed it on that "carny" existence, show business. My father would have a weekend "visitation" with my sisters where he gave them a twenty-dollar bill and dropped them off in Westwood (where movies played and UCLA stood) for twelve hours while he spent time with his new spouse and son.

The oldest younger sister met her future husband there. He parked cars and was twice her age. She craved attention – someone to love her. She was stuck with a mother who noticed her younger sister more and a father who watched his own steps but couldn't figure out what to do with or for his two daughters. The older sister told the younger sister to not tell their mother about her admirer and their weekly twelve-hour outings in the college town.

Our stepmother, with her usual malice, later called my oldest sister a "streetwalker" when she found out she had a boyfriend.

It wasn't until a few years later that my mother found out what this court-ordered visitation really amounted to and she pulled the plug. My parents still spoke on the telephone occasionally and saw each other when my father picked up my sisters. It was awkward to see them in the same space now, and uncomfortable for all of us.

During one memorable occasion, my father and stepmother were going out of town on a business/pleasure trip and they couldn't find a house sitter. My father offered the opportunity to my oldest sister who jumped at the thought of getting away from her mother for a spell. My father told my sister to set up in their bedroom while they were on the road. When my sister walked into their bedroom she was greeted with numerous photographs of all sizes featuring our stepmother au natural in various poses.

My sister's laughter turned to tears. Why had our father left our mother to spend his life with a sociopath? Was it true love or was our father flogging himself over his past deeds? Was the former altar boy evil and only deserving of his equal?

At the same time, my mother and stepfather vacationed in Hawaii and my mother introduced him to New York City and southern Connecticut. He introduced her to Boyle Heights.

Their prime location became Santa Barbara. Less than an hour and a half from the Valley, Santa Barbara was their tempo – no rush, easy, mild weather, and no children.

My mother could wear her Capris and my stepfather his Hawaiian shirts. Decision-making was always a challenge for my mother, whereas, my stepfather was in no rush, which always helped guide him toward the right decision. He had listened to my father on the radio and had laughed at the merriment and humor but that business was alien to him. Speed, showing off, being loud and drawing attention to oneself were the antithesis of his background and the manner in which he presented himself to the business world at large.

He was cool, calm, and utilized a winning smile to finish a comment or observation. My stepfather allayed all our fears of another relationship misfortune for our mother. He became the voice of reason spiritually and financially. My father never spent much time on making decisions - time was money, timing was laughter. My stepfather enjoyed closing the deal but the bottom line had to be right, it had to make sense.

In time, my oldest sister began to pull away, separate, from my father. She said "no" for the first time in her life during this time. She didn't need to win approval, to please her parents, anymore. She declined a trip to Chicago where our father was performing. My youngest sister and I said "yes."

It was hot and humid and everywhere we went the sound of KC and the Sunshine Band or Captain and Tennille prevailed, drifting on the wind. We came into contact with an authentic streetwalker who entered the hotel room we were sharing with our father in the dead of night and removed his wallet. The three of us slept soundly. This was in the day of having an actual key joining a door handle lock and releasing it. The hotel management had a list of regulars and, with the help of the Chicago Police Department, located the perpetrator, and my father's wallet was eventually returned, minus the cash.

I couldn't imagine this happening to my stepfather. My father double-locked his door as a result. When my sister and I returned home, our stepmother accused my sister of "sleeping" with her father.

Again, her crazy malice and irrational jealousy. Was she projecting her own experiences on to my sister?

In the mid seventies, I co-produced a short comedy film with a friend and booked it at a theater in Westwood playing "Dog Day Afternoon." In the days of a major film opening at one theater, there were lines around the block to see Al Pacino in his new film. I couldn't wait for my father to return home to show him my film in front of a live audience. The manager of the theater and I had an agreement where I could see the short film without paying admission.

I persuaded my father to attend the two minutes of attempted humor. I was nervous. There was only one performer in our family and he would be watching his kid, the only "actor" on screen, in front of a thousand patrons.

We parked and walked toward the theater. A few people in line murmured as we approached the entrance - clearly they recognized the comedy star on their television sets every night in syndication. The manager almost tripped over himself as he came face to face with my guest, the famous actor. Hands were shaken while I was invisible for the moment, something I was used to.

We picked out two centrally located seats and waited while the audience was assembling. My armpits were moist. I wasn't trying to invade my father's territory. I wasn't an actor nor did I want to be unlike my youngest sister who thought her father would open doors and arrange meetings for her.

My co-producer and I invested $1,600 of our hard-earned money in a camera operator, his assistant, a camera rental, and film. There was no wiggle room for an actor so I performed the role. The goal was to make the piece pay off with a large punchline laugh at the end. The lights went down. Coming attractions were next. We were reminded that Mann Theatres was presenting the program, then there was silence and darkness.

I felt like an anxiety attack was approaching. Our short film began. There was a chuckle here and there as the audience tried to anticipate what was coming. I stole a quick glance at my father who at least wasn't reading *Variety* like he did at Dodger games. The two minutes raced to the conclusion. Another titter then, bang, a tremendous roar of laughter. I smiled internally. I didn't want to get a big head. We got up from our chairs making our way out through the darkness before Al Pacino's latest film began.

As we left the theater and walked to the car, not a single question was asked about the film: how much did it cost, where did you film it, how did you come up with the idea, why were you in it? My father had to hustle home to help his wife with some pressing issue she had. We separated.

I gave an "atta boy" pat on my own shoulder and let out an internal vociferous yell: 'Good job! Way to go! The audience loved it! I can't wait to see your next film!' Everything my father's fragile ego would not allow him to say.

I put that experience in storage and retreated from the notion of ever trying to please others again. I learned to satisfy myself, first. The act of creating an idea was internal, private, and fortuitous. The fact that my father didn't exclaim superlatives like a proud parent was supplanted by his chant over the years of the importance of gaining "experience." Perhaps he witnessed that his son had and felt no need to be redundant. Still, behaving like a wounded puppy, I would have gladly received any oral pats on the back from him.

My stepfather and I started to have breakfast at least once a week at the country club affiliated with the development where he sold homes, or at the public golf course in the Sepulveda Basin, a recreational area in the Valley. I had breakfast with my father infrequently, in which he would pour ketchup on his eggs and never drink coffee.

My stepfather and I drank a lot of coffee.

He tried to involve me in golf with trips to a nearby 3-par 9-hole facility but to no success. I was awful and I wouldn't take lessons. He hit medium length drives but down the middle every time. We attended USC football games and spent many hours at Dodger Stadium watching baseball, together.

He was a good guy. But I felt guilty for liking him. We were learning from each other – he had never had stepchildren and I had never had a stepfather. We learned détente. We compromised. My stepfather and I placed my mother's happiness near the top, and we had *that* in common.

My stepfather took his time. He was never in a rush. My father was always in a rush. My stepfather drank beer and liked to barbecue. My father almost never drank and my mother was always in charge of flipping the hamburgers.

My stepfather worked in the yard. My father paid a gardener. My stepfather was an Air Force veteran. So was my father – on television. My stepfather enjoyed Clint Eastwood action movies. My father liked light comedies with Jack Lemmon. They never would have known each other except for my father's guilt, which drove him to search for a new home for his ex-wife and their three children that my stepmother naturally opposed, in every way.

My oldest sister never had a proper relationship with our mother who never seemed to listen to her and had a hard time connecting with her. My sister's memory of our mother began at age four as my sister clung to our grandmother's dress as she looked with trepidation at our mother as the mean lady who would come around but was not particularly loving towards her.

After our parents' divorce when my sister was ten years old, she observed an argument between our mother and grandmother. Our mother observed my sister wearing a fearful expression that something would happen to our grandmother. Our mother raised her right hand and screamed at my sister: "I should never have had you!" That verbal attack affects my sister to this day. Cruel words can never be unsaid.

Our youngest sister who received most of our mother's attention years later started to dissect relationships in our family and apologized to her sister for always taking our mother's side – "I'm sorry for being mad at you. Now, I know what you've been going through," she told her older sister.

Our grandmother shared with us that since childhood our mother never listened to her and often told her not to tell her what to do. Our grandmother's other daughter who was older than our mother often remained quiet during these moments not wanting to interfere.

My oldest younger sister says she tried to be a good daughter even though she was treated like a second-class citizen. She had a loud machine gun delivery and wild sense of humor like our father while the youngest sister was tentative and indecisive like our mother. I would have thought that my oldest sister's behavior reminded my mother of her first love, my father. But, depending on the day, that comparison came with a weight that could submerge all good memories, sinking them to the ocean floor. My oldest sister was my father's daughter through no fault of her own. We choose friends not families.

My father and stepmother were once on a business/pleasure trip to New York City, and a first, to visit the former in-laws (my mother's sister and brother-in-law) in Connecticut. I volunteered to housesit but there were no nude photographs of my stepmother on display this time around.

I spent time in the back room watching videos and playing audiotapes. One day, mid-morning I received a phone call from my mother. My father's father was dead. He had died of a massive heart attack, his heart exploded, which resulted in blood all over my grandparents' home. Would I call her sister's home and inform my father who was visiting? I felt badly for my grandmother although I didn't cry. I spoke to my aunt who passed me over to my father who then took the phone. I had never informed someone of a death and it was awkward.

There was an audible release from my father like "Awwwww" as he began to replay his relationship with his father in his mind. There was silence, and then insignificant verbal exchanges such as when I said: "I'm sorry dad." We hung up a few moments later.

Both my grandfathers were now deceased. My father's father had held his wife hostage for decades – no friends allowed, don't talk with the neighbors, he would go to the mailbox and collect the mail, he would take out the trash, he would wait in the hair salon while his wife was being attended to, he told her what to wear, how to act, and what to say.

I always thought she must have felt great relief and freedom when he breathed his last breath. She was free – almost. Her oldest son soon reappeared after the smoke had cleared, drinking, going through packs of cigarettes, arguing with his younger brother, and singing for no one's pleasure.

My mother sold the old modern where she had lived and pooled her capital gain with my stepfather's funds to build their own home on a hill overlooking the Valley. There were hawks overhead, coyotes on the street and wild rabbits scampering around in the yard. The home was simply laid out sans pool with a Jacuzzi instead. And it was theirs.

Soon after the move, a new phase began with the ex-family 'get togethers.' My father, his mother, and his brother, my mother, grandmother, sisters and stepfather would sit around the kitchen table with coffee and pastries nostalgically discussing the past – friends, family from Connecticut – while laughing over the hour and a half visit.

My stepfather was quiet, surveilling the unique situation before him. He loved my mother and would do anything for her. My mother's sister called during one of the meetings, with my mother announcing: "You'll never guess who's here." My mother stretched the moment for maximum effect. Finally, with delight, she reeled off the roster of players. Her sister then retorted, "Only in Hollywood."

I wanted to be Steven Spielberg. I wanted to make another short film. I wanted a thousand moviegoers in line for the next Warren Beatty opening to view my work, too. My father was out of town, performing his play in Teaneck, New Jersey, or El Paso, Texas, and out of the blue, my stepmother invited me to the house for dinner. She made a strip steak and baked potato meal to be consumed at the kitchen nook table. She had had a few glasses of red wine and a couple of cigarettes by the time I arrived. We ate and talked. It seemed innocent enough.

Then she proudly told me about her sexual conquests with actors Mike Connors, Bill Cosby and Frank Sinatra. I listened to her jaw-dropping Hollywood tales as though I were her 'in awe' baby brother. I chose the right moment to pitch a film idea about a desert diner where she would play a waitress in lust with the proverbial road cowboy. She smiled.

There would be a steamy scene where her blouse gets torn. "I wouldn't mind if you saw my breasts," said my stepmother, staring at me and burning a hole between my eyes. I looked down at the remnants of my dinner, waited a few seconds and changed the subject. I kept thinking, 'I wouldn't mind seeing my stepmother's ample breasts' but she *was* my stepmother, and off limits.

The awkward situation felt like a stock movie of the week starring Victoria Principal. It also felt like another move on my stepmother's lifelike game of chess. If I had pursued the clumsy invitation for a few seconds of abandon she may have cried "Rape!" to my father, and eliminated another first family member, checking me off her list.

Or, she may have waited for his return and another opportunity at a live tribunal where my relationship with my father could have been shattered, destroyed, another familial connection severed. That was who she was - that was what she was about, happiest when she could place another proverbial notch on the belt, and destroy another relationship, with a smile and a shrug.

There were always mental games and tests of loyalty. I talked about filmmaking and we chatted about her appearance in my father's play in Chicago – what it was like to work with one's spouse. The evening ended, I thanked her for dinner, kissed her on the cheek and left never to mention the desert diner short film idea again.

I had refused to fall into her trap.

Miles and miles of driving around Los Angeles with my father in control of the vehicle but not much else – career stalled, television and movies having lost interest, his hour and a half standup comedy play and the occasional radio appearances were paying the bills. Even the former television star becoming a curiosity for a few weeks in cities such as Columbus, Ohio, had run its course. The thrill was gone.

As my father drove, I, his audience of one, listened to his complaints about career and home life but did not have the self-confidence or experience – the balls - to add my opinions and comments about his mid-life crisis. I sat silent and just listened. We stopped for hamburgers, dropped off film to be processed and picked up show business trade papers to read about the roles he didn't get. The disappointment and lack of forward motion were not discussed, but they were felt.

I could not criticize his career decisions or lack of self-promotion – the parties or ads in Variety and Hollywood Reporter. Who was I, the co-maker of a two-minute short film and co-writer of a film book, to analyze a once vibrant career that was now rapidly speeding downhill?

At home, my father had substantial disagreements with my stepmother that developed into arguments that would last for days and weeks mainly emanating from her endless toxic hatred of his original family members - my mother, sisters, my father's mother, and me.

Her lacerating comments hurt him not to mention the ashtrays, lamps and videotape boxes thrown at him with a sporadic direct hit. He would appear on stage in Jacksonville, Florida, with a split lip or a facial bruise. During one memorable scuffle, my father announced to my stepmother in my presence that even his son couldn't fathom how he could elect to stay with her. "Even Bobby doesn't understand why I'm staying with you!"

She turned from my father and focused her laser stare of hatred at me. I felt the floor split open beneath my feet. I was now terminated, another first family dismemberment. I was a living ghost like the other kin. Thank you father.

My mother had "Love from this day forward" engraved on my stepfather's wedding ring. There was love in the air, a successful bond between two people seeking peace and happiness. My stepfather had a backbone and a simple, direct, honest perception of right and wrong.

At my youngest sister's high school graduation party at my mother and stepfather's home, my father and stepfather sat next to each other in the backyard looking out over the Valley. They talked quietly, in almost intimate brotherly tones with periodic laughter.

The rest of the family left them alone for what seemed like an hour. No one dared interrupt the historic meeting. They were getting along, enjoying each other's company. Later, my stepfather would share with me that my father had told him that he "never should have left" my mother "and the kids."

How did my stepfather react? He listened intently to my father and let him share his personal observations on his own failed union. My stepfather took in the remarks and processed them, behaving like a friend listening to someone's confessed imperfections and shortcomings. My stepfather looked my father in the eyes with strength and steadiness and integrity. And it was clear, my father felt safe putting forth these admissions knowing my stepfather would absorb the report and not use the information in the perverted way that my stepmother *would* have done.

My father shared that he was "seeing the color orange for the first time", taking a breath and removing the horse blinders he'd been wearing for so long.

He would be changing course in the next months ahead. He would be trying to navigate the mid-life crisis in play. He was two weeks shy of fifty. My stepfather was six months his senior on a steady course capable of spotting white caps ahead and sailing clear of them in an understated manner. My stepfather removed stress from my mother's life. She loved her new husband but she also loved her ex-husband, that I knew would never change.

My stepfather grew up on the east side of downtown Los Angeles in Boyle Heights when there was a considerable population of what he called "white Russians." He hustled like the next kid. His father provided a small salary earned as a postal worker, his mother was deaf and didn't work, and there was no family savings. So, hustle he did.

My stepfather put together a shoeshine kit and hit the pavement. First stop: Mister Lasky who owned the neighborhood convenience store. My stepfather offered to shine his black shoes for ten cents. That was too much. Five cents. Okay. My stepfather asked, "Which shoe do you want shined?"

Another divorce was imminent for my father. It was obvious, as they were that unhappy.

He moved out of his latest home and shared an apartment with me. I would watch over his mass of electronic equipment. This included video recorders, hi-fi equipment, thousands of record albums and video and still cameras while he was on the road working hard to earn money to pay for his latest predicament.

We talked on my 27th birthday and he announced further developments: he was going to purchase a home when he returned to Los Angeles in a few weeks and he was concluding a friendship with the video equipment salesperson, who would visit him in various cities such as Traverse City, Michigan, to share nightlife with the B celebrity, my Dad.

Willy Loman was tired. He wanted to create changes in his life. He was seeing the "color orange" after all and had begun to sense liberation was in the air.

After several years, my mother and her ex-mother-in-law were on speaking terms. My grandmother disliked her latest daughter-in-law, "the actress" and preferred her previous one with a new appreciation. I picked up my grandmother and drove her to the Valley to spend a few hours with my mother and stepfather.

As we arrived at their home, my stepfather approached us, his infectious smile absent. He directed me to call my father's attorney who, once on the phone, asked if I would like to accompany him to Phoenix.

My father had been shot.

I turned to the assembled family – my mother, my stepfather, sisters, and grandmothers - in the kitchen. I quietly announced what I had just heard. There was instant bedlam. There were screams, moans and bursts of tears and grief. I would update them from Arizona, I told them, as I turned around and fled out the front door.

The year was 1978 and I was 27-years-old.

By the time I reported back to my family, my father had been dead for over twelve hours – not shot but bludgeoned to death, we later found out. My stepfather answered the telephone. I told him as unemotionally as I could that I had seen my father's body at the morgue. It would be my stepfather's job to inform the room. I could only imagine what that would be like but a part of me was glad I would not be there.

Hours later, I sat by a motel pool drinking beer in the hundred-degree heat. My father had been altering his life but there were two prominent obstacles, a cruel second wife who had the motive, and my father's definition of a friend who had the means and opportunity to take his life from him.

These two players were being shuffled out of the deck.

My stepfather later described to me the wailing in the kitchen as ongoing with each woman present replaying memories from decades ago, *and* from last week. My stepfather replayed his recent conversation with my father – the longest conversation they would have – where my stepfather played the priest in the confession booth to his lost member of the flock.

My stepfather was calm and steady all through this.

I spoke with Scottsdale Police Department homicide detectives and their take was that the homicide of my father was a crime of passion and not a break-in robbery gone askew. I returned to Los Angeles and the apartment I shared with my father only to find a hired guard in the employ of my stepmother blocking the front door. I showed the guard my apartment key and negotiated with my stepmother's attorney to be allowed in since I lived there and my clothing and possessions were in my bedroom. The embarrassed custodian spent the night on the couch in the living room as I passed the hours in my own bed trying unsuccessfully to fall asleep.

The next morning my stepmother arrived to survey the apartment to see how her estranged husband had been living for the past six months. She made mental notes of electronic equipment, photographs and any telltale signs of female cohabitation. I watched her and listened in silence. I didn't know what to say. The air had been sucked out of the flat.

To fill the silence I innocently asked: "Why did this have to happen?" Not missing a beat, my stepmother explained with indifference that the murder occurred because the lifestyle of my father – her husband - had caught up with him. I had no comeback. She wanted to move on from this space immediately and cut her losses. She never mentioned her own role as cheating mistress in her lofty judgment of my father.

I had a day to evacuate, taking with me a videotape deck, a monitor, an audio tape recorder and my father's military uniform from the World War Two television series. In a moment of weakness, I left the hat behind because my stepmother wanted it for her son. Without my father's presence, the clothing was nothing more than a rental off the racks of Western Costume in Hollywood, but it still meant something to *me*.

I closed the apartment door for the last time. The six months living with my father had been a final opportunity to see him daily for weeks at a time enjoying his humor and lightness through this dry season – a break-up with his second wife, separation from his newest son, attorneys, the prospect of court, an unstable career, the roller coaster ride of fame to a future of obscurity and, for this actor, the sense of time lost forever.

A gathering was held at my mother and stepfather's home where only a few weeks previous my father and stepfather had had their man-to-man chat. Neighbors, relatives and a few business associates of my stepfather, some making their first and only appearances at the home, spent time imbibing and enjoying the view of the Valley saying the awkward and hollow words well meaning people always say after a death.

Some people expected celebrities, but there were none. They stayed away. After everyone left, my family didn't mention my father, the death or murder. We cleaned up as if a birthday party had just taken place – a rare celebration.

My UnHollywood Family

My father's funeral was held on the Westside with my family and my stepmother's family, friends and a few television celebrities attending. My father's brother wearing sunglasses was there, relieved he had his mother's full attention now and forever. My family avoided my stepmother, her daughter and her son, my half-brother who would never know me.

The prime suspect in my father's murder, the video equipment salesperson, and an old hanger on of my father's, walked over to me and embraced me. He would treat me as a trusted confidant for a month until the Scottsdale Police Department turned up the heat and his attorney suggested he not speak to anyone, most of all members of the deceased actor's family.

My mother was shedding tears for her high school sweetheart and the father of her three children. She held hands with my stepfather. My stepmother lost future income but would more than make up for the loss by cashing in two life insurance policies on my father and selling their Westwood home. As my stepfather would describe one of his real estate properties, "triple net."

My father was buried near his father in an ordinary north Valley cemetery.

Allegedly, Fred Astaire and Ginger Rogers are buried there, too. I do not visit grounds containing decaying bodies in overly expensive containers. I prefer photographs and memories to staring at a plaque in a patch of under-watered crabgrass.

My youngest sister preferred the in-person visit. On her third trip, she noticed fresh overturned soil and the plaque missing. She visited the cemetery office. Our father's remains had been moved and the office worker had been directed to not inform visitors of his whereabouts. My youngest sister demanded that the office worker place a phone call to the contact of record.

Our stepmother's attorney finally relented and gave my youngest sister a new location: the modish center of Westwood where my father lay among celebrities. The shiny plaque complete with photographs of my father and stepmother mentioned children from each parent except *me*.

My stepmother would share the plot when the time came. Her sexy likeness conveyed an abundance of cleavage. I have never visited the site. I have witnessed its Hollywood cheapness from the Internet.

The ostentatious gravesite is a monument to a relationship that would have died had my father lived, but lived on *because* he died.

Within a few weeks, I was summoned to Santa Monica Courthouse to stand trial for misappropriating the items from the apartment. I took the stand and was grilled by my stepmother's attorney. My defense was that my father passed on the equipment to his loving oldest son. I turned to my left and watched the judge reading paperwork seemingly oblivious to the hardcore interrogation. The judge was bored and clearly behaved as if this case was unimportant and not worthy of his judgeship and courtroom's time. The case was ultimately dismissed.

I found out later that the attorney hit my stepmother's wallet hard.

My father's attorney informed me I was going to receive money.

The six thousand dollar payout was established during my parents' days together when I was a youngster. It had nothing to do with his will which was rewritten not long before his death adding a codicil that effectively terminated his three children from his first marriage.

Again, I thought of motive. My father's soon-to-be-ex-wife seized everything monetarily speaking. The motive? Money.

I cashed the check, rented a 35-millimeter camera, lights and bought film and produced another comedy short film this time about an older couple trying to make their second marriages work. No role for my stepmother. I booked the nine minute piece in another Westwood theatre – no lines around the block waiting to see Pacino. Instead, a smattering of Richard Dreyfuss followers watching an underperforming feature and short film. I wouldn't have to worry about my father's reaction this time.

My oldest sister got married at twenty to the parking lot attendant she had courted in Westwood. Our mother wasn't happy. Retracing her own steps, our mother tried to make the point that getting married young automatically leads to divorce. Again, we were not the type of family where anyone got cheered on. My mother couldn't say anything nice about my oldest sister. She would endlessly pick on her. Later, when my oldest sister had two boys a few years apart, she avoided our mother instead visiting our paternal grandmother who commented that she was a wonderful mother and meant to be a mother.

Those kinds of supportive words never emanated from our mother. There were only negative comments about my oldest sister's hair, weight, changing apartments so often, *and* her tattoos.

My sister's boys would grow up to be independent and industrious, my mother not aware of the in's and out's of their daily lives let alone their make-up and characteristics that she just never knew about them and that my oldest sister chose never to share. She and her husband would divorce years down the road, with my oldest sister proclaiming her most noteworthy accomplishment as co-producing two self-reliant sons.

There was an abundance of divorce in our family: our parents, our stepfather and his first wife, my oldest sister, and, eventually, my youngest sister would add three to the total.

Our mother surprised my oldest sister during a hospital stay where my oldest sister had had gallbladder and breast cyst surgeries. She was withdrawing from five days of a morphine drip, sweating, not knowing her own name and wanting to jump out the window to the parking lot below. The nurse yelled at my sister to calm down as our mother entered the room. The nurse was rude and short with my sister. Our mother heard and saw how the nurse was behaving and shouted at the nurse to do her job. Who did she think she was? The nurse was scared of our mother at that point and gave my sister Valium. She thought she would lose her job. The next day, the nurse sat down on the bed beside my sister and apologized for being impatient.

My mother confronting the nurse was a rare act of aggression, but it also demonstrated her love for my sister. My mother was comfortable around doctors and considered a hospital a safe place. Her energy level rose that unordinary day. My mother never jumped out of bed, put on her sneakers, ran a 5K, on the way home picked flowers for an arrangement, and whipped up a flapjack breakfast with freshly squeezed orange juice for the family. That was not my mother.

She had courage that day as she reprimanded the nurse for bullying my sister. After all, she was a veteran of three births and a miscarriage, hepatitis, an appendectomy, esophageal complications, and, later, hip replacement and open-heart surgery, no cancer.

Outside of her bed at home, hospitals offered a comfort zone. She knew talented doctors from bad, a kindly genuine bedside manner from a non-existent one, caring support staff from just punching a time card. If my mother had had a job, working in the hospitality trade would have offered the client my mother at her prime. It was dealing with her family that perplexed her.

The era of "fuck" bombs exploding within four walls and ashtrays being flung to make a point ended at my father and stepmother's home. She had ruled the roost in that relationship and, despite being mentioned occasionally at the police department and district attorney's offices in Arizona, the doyenne of the mock Tudor dwelling atop the Westwood hills was flush with cash and single again.

My stepmother's attorney pounded home the alibi that his client and her young son had been in Seattle during my father's murder. The fact that his client and her son had paid an unannounced surprise visit to my father's guest quarters in Arizona ten days *before* his demise and a recently modified will containing a codicil dismissing my father's children from his previous marriage, with his dubious signature affixed didn't persuade let alone interest the authorities to take a serious look at the soon-to-be ex-wife who had gained financially from her estranged husband's death, before the divorce my father wanted could even happen.

Not bad for an actress who couldn't convincingly deliver a line of dialogue. Not bad for an actress who was at the bottom of the production call sheet to seduce and capture number one on the list of players. My stepmother soon purchased a handgun only weeks after my father's murder. Why? She was *certain* someone was observing her every movement, tallying the numbers, me perhaps? This is what I heard.

I would never come face to face with her again. My volleys would be words delivered through any member of the press who cared to listen or wanted a great quote for their newspaper or magazine.

My stepmother was dusk, the end of the day, a cigarette, a glass of red wine, another cigarette, another glass, until she sat in a somber setting void of illumination, alone, the commander of her death squad, the designer of dread for the living. What was the endgame? Who was the winner of her twisted chess game, the pieces played by humans?

My gullible pawn of a father who never should have been married, played first with someone beneath his playing skills, humoring her for decades while searching for a stronger player, a challenger, someone to humble him, someone to call checkmate.

He found her. She survived, he didn't.

The coffee klatch at my mother and stepfather's home was now less one participant. My parents' relationship had evolved into a brother/sister kinship with the memory of proclaiming love for the first time to someone outside the family. My stepfather and his ex-wife slipped into similar roles. Both men departed their homes with only their clothing and automobiles (and electronic equipment). Both ex-couples found out that the American Dream of home ownership, material wealth and a swimming pool was essentially an empty pursuit that did not lead to happiness.

Both ex-couples spun their wheels, throwing blame for failure in unions that started too early in their lives before they had any clue who they were, or how they had gotten there. They were told by television commercials that their visions and yearnings were indeed within their grasp. But once they packed and moved, unloaded and sorted the kitchenware, the dresses and suits, the tools and make-up, that chapter of their story ended.

Television commercials aren't responsible for promoting happy flourishing alliances. They are responsible for moving products.

My stepfather was the father of the bride four times and father of the groom twice. All the brides' marriages have ended with divorce. I married twice with my first wife departing after ten years with metastatic breast cancer. I have been married for twenty-four years to my present wife. She and her ex-husband divorced after his dalliances terminated *her* trust and hope.

I have a stepdaughter, son-in-law, stepgrandson and stepgranddaughter. I succumbed to self-imposed pressure regarding my first marriage when my best friends met their mates and unionized. They were officially adults. I was still an immature searcher, looking for my reason for living. My first wife was an adventurer of creativity and of structure. She designed yards, wrote stories and made quirky drawings. She would grow tired of my kicking and screaming as I fought the notion of becoming an adult.

I was afraid of buying into the American Dream, purchasing the home and car and backyard barbecue and discovering that the dream was hollow. There would be no divorce though because her enterprising projects and exploits would rapidly fade to dread as her youthfulness transitioned into helplessness despite my best efforts and the cancer consumed her.

Sadness had struck again in my life.

I retreated from adulthood until I met a wise and kind mother of a five-year-old who was seeking truth and commitment from a partner. She wanted a demarcation line, a fresh start. She didn't want her and her daughter to live with me unless we were married, setting some kind of example of solidarity for her child.

I would set the pursuit of adulthood aside and concentrate on being honest, forthcoming and present with two human beings. My first marriage ceremony took place in Santa Barbara. We exchanged simple bands from a Native American craft store. My second marriage ceremony transpired in Maui. We exchanged a band of small encased diamonds for her and a silver and platinum band for me.

My father missed it all: marriages, births and deaths.

Years later, I was working for an actor who could make you laugh and cry. I had interviewed him so many times for magazines and newspapers that he trusted me as his liaison to the press. I set up interviews for the upcoming week and canceled them on Monday morning after he emptied a jug of rum over the weekend.

My stepfather and I had a G job as this actor's right hand man would refer to tasks undertaken for the benefit of the performer. We would fly to Durango, Mexico, and set up living accommodations for a three-month film shoot. We flew via Puerto Vallarta where we consumed a basket of tortilla chips and a bowl of guacamole alongside five or six beers each. In Durango, we caught a cab that tilted to the right and sat in the back seat which was covered by a horse blanket as the springs had busted through the seat fabric.

Keeping in mind that the actor was rotund, smoked, and Durango sat seven thousand feet above sea level we secured a single story home with plenty of area for guests. The dwelling overlooked a public park where gunfire could be heard after the sun had set.

We stayed at the most pleasant hotel in town where the lovely local women lunched. We dined at the best restaurant where we ordered fajitas. Expecting the Southern California presentation a la Casa Vega in the Valley, we were taken aback by a lonesome plate containing strips of flank steak and nothing more. Where were the chips and guac, rice, and beans? We weren't in SoCal anymore.

I accompanied the actor and his posse – the Chongos – back to Durango. He spent ten miserable weeks performing an underwritten script guided by a director that didn't know what to do with him. Tequila took top billing, gunshots were heard, driving back to the hotel at three in the morning was an adventure and three million dollars were put in the actor's coffers. Still, despondency, even gloom, overtook the job.

I was back in Los Angeles when one morning at seven o'clock I received word from the right hand man that the actor who released filmgoers' emotions, which conjured laughter and tears, was dead. He died literally putting his boots on.

I called my stepfather who would rise at five, and we linked up by the 405 Freeway and hot tailed it to the actor's widow to deliver the life-changing news before the media did. My stepfather and I arrived at the actor's compound at eight o'clock. We rang the doorbell. The actor's wife opened the door. As no words were exchanged, she studied our faces and just knew, then emitted a shriek. We held her, wordless, just sobbing. At eight-thirty the media broke the story.

The death cycle continued with the passing of my father's mother. She had had heart problems followed by surgery, a risk for any older patient. Her troubled elder son had shared an apartment with her in her last years, his drinking and smoking not to mention his renditions of Sinatra tunes only adding to her angst. She had a slight frame and a contagious laugh. My grandmother lived to her early nineties. The comedic aspect of her passing was that the one person who abused himself the most of the four family members was the survivor and outlived her, her oldest son.

I never saw or spoke to my uncle again. When he eventually died, he left the money he received from my grandmother to a fellow war veteran I had never known.

My father didn't miss his murder trial. His presence permeated the county courthouse in Arizona. The video salesperson and hanger on was on trial – means and opportunity. I filled the witness chair for a portion of a day describing my father's purported rejection of this friend as the fuse for the brutal revenge killing. My father had wanted to move on, his rejected "friend" didn't want him to.

Videotapes containing X-rated home movies starring my father, his then-comrade, the former friend, and miscellaneous eager female co-stars naturally became the prominent articles of evidence. The jurors shriveled, embarrassed collectively for the once famous television actor. I attempted several times to make eye contact with jurors to no avail. They refused even to look at me.

They were uncomfortable for me trying to make sense of my father's life in a public courtroom. They probably felt badly for me too. I was young, just a kid really. My stepfather accompanied me to the trial. I was mortified that he heard and saw his wife's ex-husband – my father – in total abandon before a camera, becoming a frat house pledge on speed. The videos put my father on tiral and seemed to blame him for being murdered. An early example of victim-blaming.

My stepfather and I would converse for hours about the unsolved case: motivation, deception, witnesses, location, dialogue, timing, friends, lovers, and my father's vindictive estranged wife. Upon conclusion of my fruitless appearance for the prosecution, my stepfather and I, dripping with perspiration, walked back to the hotel and consumed the best cheeseburgers and schooners of cold beer that we'd ever had.

Over the years I learned that my stepfather was epileptic and prone to occasional seizures in public. This might occur at banks, super markets, restaurants and even the golf course. Amazingly, he was never embarrassed and spoke about epilepsy openly. I was present for one seizure at home. He would grow quiet losing concentration then his body would succumb to a fit of violent shaking.

The time I was present my mother and I got him on his side on the floor and rode it out with him. After a minute his body relaxed and his concentration returned as if he had just woken up from a nap. The grogginess would rapidly fade and he would be present again. We were always thankful that the seizures didn't transpire when he was behind the wheel. He was a commercial and residential property landlord – automobiles and humans. He loved talking with people and solving problems. He traveled the Valley. At one point, the Department of Motor Vehicles put his driver's license on suspension for a year but nevertheless he drove. He required control to be happy in life.

Weeks later into the trial, the Public Defender got his client off. The video salesperson walked free and spent the next four years (his last) at home with a wife the courtroom learned about for the first time. Then a heart attack. He left behind a grown son the courtroom learned about for the first time as well.

The son would take the stand and tell the courtroom about his father's anger issues. The video salesperson studied karate to temper his outbursts. At the time of his death, video also died on a national scale. Everyone had a cell phone, by then. Everyone recorded sex. Everyone shared exploits with everyone else.

One of the most considerate things my youngest sister ever did for me was to call me to give me a heads up regarding my maternal grandmother's physical condition. She was ninety-three, her sturdy Swedish stock finally giving out. When I arrived at her rest home, she was breathing, her eyelids closed. From Helsingborg, Sweden, on a ship to America to work as a domestic worker, to meeting her future husband to giving birth to two daughters, to widowhood to son-in-laws who were kind-hearted, to grandchildren, to the Valley.

I held her hand and whispered: "Thank you for being so selfless and benevolent with us kids." I hoped she heard me. I sat with her for a few hours and kissed her on the cheek. I studied her face one last time. The lines were deep, her complexion pale, her short grey hair uncombed. I thanked the staff and held my tears until I left the building. My grandmother died that night.

Two decades after my father's death, with the internet informing the population, my demented stepmother and her son created a website to share my father's not for sale videos and still photograph archives. Box loads of material offering nudes and X-rated images were marketed on-line. T-shirts displaying my father in a sex act were for sale—such a loving tribute to a husband and father.

My stepmother's rage toward, resentment and envy of a once successful actor playing an admired role that would live on for decades tore apart any sensible judgment she might have had regarding her own son's remaining memories of his late father or even her son's mental health. I knew my father for twenty-seven years. His younger son knew him for only seven years, and likely doesn't even remember him.

My stepmother's passionate wrath of all things pertaining to my father continued, when on commercial television she told the interviewer of a weekly network news program that my father treated women like "toilet paper." The fact that my stepmother avoided a divorce and garnered all the money and property was not enough for her. She was inflamed that people whispered about marital difficulties and murder behind her back even though the police investigators didn't. Her personal war with my father had been simmering for years. There were unique outlets now offering new audiences for her to persuade of his rottenness. Conversely, she also declared how happy they were.

She would never know the responsibility or stress of being "number one" on the film production call sheet. She was playing an impossibly quirky role now – herself. Mass audiences wouldn't open their arms. My stepmother needed a good director, but she would not find one.

In the early 2000s I learned that the writer of "Taxi Driver" loved my father's storyline: former Catholic altar boy grows up in a small town at odds with his father, goes to Hollywood where his sinful wicked ways are encouraged to surface and flourish, destroying marriages, using women particularly as fodder in his quest to fill his ego, all while his work topples and he faces the reality that he will never be iconic like the fictional role he portrayed.

The writer was beside himself making a film about "a person who was bad from the beginning, a person whose level of hypocrisy went down with his first marriage and he became more of the person he always was."

My stepmother, who was hawking her late estranged husband's pornographic collection online, came to his rescue opposing the production of the film. The script presented her as a day-drinking, pathetic, violent home-wrecker, and that, being too close to the truth, infuriated her.

I told the *New York Times* that she was the only person to profit from his death and that the police and district attorney's office should take a closer look at her. I compared my stepmother to con artist/murderer Sante Kimes *and* Adolf Hitler.

I was then slapped with a cease and desist order.

My stepmother insisted there was no money involved, that "the TV show hadn't kicked into syndication yet" [after thirteen years playing on televisions all over the world] and that "the estate was worth nothing." She further stated that she "loved [her] husband and [they] were reconciled at the time of his death." Pure fiction.

All lies.

Then why was I at the apartment I shared with my father when I received a telephone call from the video salesman asking me if "everything" was "alright" just hours before my father was declared a murder victim? His tone was flat. He didn't sound like he normally did.

My mother merely tolerated the entertainment industry when she was married to my father but now she had the time to lunch with one of her favorite actresses who just happened to be portraying her in the film about my father's life.

The actress wanted to study her face and movements and her speech patterns. My mother wanted to inspect the actress' skin and have a laugh with her. I drove my mother to the luncheon. After a few hours, I received a call from her. The meeting was ending and the actress and my mother were best friends.

The actress looked and sounded like my mother in the film. They never saw each other again.

Later, my mother, stepfather, wife and I ran into the director of the film at a famous old Hollywood restaurant. My stepfather had no interest in the film industry and my mother could not have cared less because this person was not a famous actor. Her facial muscles tightened as she endured his presence.

My wife and I spent an evening with the director at another classic Hollywood restaurant, a few days later, thumbing through the film script and making notes and deletions. We were spooling pasta, drinking a bold red and behaving as if we belonged to the film club. The writer of "Taxi Driver" helmed a film about my father that my father and I would definitely have stood in line in Westwood to see.

My mother, stepfather, and even my stepmother had no interest in spending an hour and forty-five minutes observing strong sexuality. This would include not wanting to see nudity, some drug use, and violence revolving around someone they had loved or been an audience for prior to the plans and promises evolving into empty words and his early demise.

Being the carefree optimist conceiving there was a "pony" hidden in every great pile of excrement, my father moved without discretion. Believing he was an innocent, and not paying attention to responsibility had paved his way to ruin.

My stepmother held that *she* was untouchable. With two marriages ending in her spouse's death, forever studying the chessboard, making moves with a cold heart, directing her decisions, cancer finally sideswiped her - catching her by surprise.

After thousands of packs of cigarettes, a simple cough turned into a bloody trail with no escape plan this time. According to her daughter from her previous union, my stepmother begged for a cigarette on her deathbed. Her gravesite had been prepared for her since my father's entombment in 1978, the engraved image with her sexy pose and low-cut dress on the plaque meant to remind visitors why my father had left my *mother*.

There were no more schemes to be hatched, no more names to be called, her wicked spiteful laughter at someone's expense passive forever. She was a kind of Nazi, with breasts, and that is how I will always remember her.

The goodbyes were becoming more frequent. The old uniform worn by my father for the World War Two television series was next. It had hung in my mother and stepfather's hallway closet for years among the dusty coats and articles of clothing from the Sixties and Seventies.

As our family never seemed to celebrate any event I felt it was time to commemorate the costume that had been observed on television by millions of viewers over decades. I released the outfit to a famous auction house with the consent of my oldest sister and the protestations of my mother and youngest sister who didn't want to part with it.

The outfit was one of the lots at the Pop Culture event in New York City. The costume sat among signed albums by the Beatles and Bob Dylan, Marlon Brando's "Godfather" script and Kurt Cobain's guitar. My father would have enjoyed being in the company of a Brando item.

My youngest sister heard a news bite on the radio about the outcome of the auction. The clothing was no longer in the possession of our family. An individual or group celebrated the costume by paying well over the house's estimate of fifteen to twenty thousand dollars. My youngest sister cried and my mother hollered at me. My stepfather had nothing to say.

My mother surprised me as a parental survivor. I had imagined her as the first of the four parents to die. I envisioned my father going strong into his nineties, and my stepmother into her eighties - my father living off of adrenaline, his endless optimism and autograph shows with my stepmother persisting with a diet of innate evil, cigarettes and the wineglass that was generally glued to her hand.

I wasn't sure about my stepfather with his epilepsy under control but still unpredictable. But, there they were, mother and stepfather, slowing down but chugging along. The Dodgers games evolved into a once a season visit to the stadium and breakfasts weren't weekly anymore. Their loss of hearing became impossible with hearing aids bought and misplaced and stepped on over the years.

It was like they didn't want to listen to their family let alone the news and the world at large. My stepfather's brilliant smile retreated into a frown or an angry look like Joe DiMaggio at the charity bocce tournament at Caesar's Palace in Las Vegas that my father and I had attended. I was excited to meet Joltin' Joe but he was unapproachable with his sour, suspicious expression, never the same man after he lost Marilyn, the "beautiful life" that had been destroyed and taken from him in 1962.

My stepfather would sometimes raise his voice at my mother, frustrated with his body and mind slowing down and his right hand shaking so forcefully he couldn't write a check any longer. He periodically screamed at my mother that her three children were "fucking losers." These outbursts scared her and she would retreat into their bedroom, giving him space to calm down. The next day my stepfather would tell my mother how much he loved her and that he couldn't live without her. Two or three days later he wouldn't talk to her all day. His behavior could be perplexing to say the least.

When we got my stepfather to a doctor he was examined and proclaimed fourth stage dementia. The condition would only get worse. My stepfather drove his car into three other cars blaming the multiple accidents on his car "taking off on its own." The story told again and again to anyone who would listen was laughable and sad as he tried to sell himself the tale using the salesmanship that he used to try to market a piece of property to a potential buyer.

His energy was no longer there. He was frustrated and incensed that he didn't buy the yarn as well. His driving days were over but my mother proudly renewed her driving license at ninety-two over the Internet due to lax Covid-related orders. She drove my stepfather now. But soon, she plowed into the wall of a deli mistaking the gas pedal for the brake pedal.

Then my stepfather fell, once at the mailbox near the street, another time on the kitchen floor where the water delivery person helped him up, and another time when he fell in the bathroom and I received a phone call from my mother. The balance of both my mother and stepfather was off, which is common with hearing loss and failing eyesight.

Still, they fought the idea of canes, walkers and wheelchairs. Their medicine-taking schedule was long and complicated; blood thinners, blood pressure, and mood stabilizers among a dozen other medications. I dreaded visiting the Walgreens pharmacy.

My stepfather sat on the den couch and watched sporting events and movies. I'd ask what he had watched. "I don't know, ask your mother," he'd say in return. I'd inquire about the names of the film's actors and actresses. "I don't know, ask your mother." I forgot that the only actor he knew by name was in fact Clint Eastwood.

My stepfather had no leg strength left and another fall turned into a 911 call, which turned into a trip to the hospital for tests. A week later he was supposed to be released. There was no cure for dementia and the doctors suggested using a walker. My stepfather wasn't wearing his hearing aids. He nodded and smiled, uncomprehending. As his catheter was being removed his eyes closed, his blood pressure rose and his left arm extended skyward. Code: stroke. My stepfather experienced an acute cerebrovascular accident. There was an operation to remove a blood clot but his fate had been determined – major irreparable brain damage affecting language and muscle function.

My wife and I stood by his bed every day trading shifts with my mother and two sisters. A week later my stepfather lay in his hospital hospice bed unattached to tubes and wires except for a hydro morphine drip. My stepfather took shallow breaths but the death mask was apparent – pale skin pulled tightly like Saran Wrap. After ninety-five years of breathing he took his last breath. My wife and I stood there like honor guards beside him, in Room 1607 on the sixth floor northeast. I called my youngest sister and delivered the sad but inevitable report. She would deliver the news to our mother in person.

My father had destroyed my family. My stepfather saved it.

A week after my stepfather's death my mother told me she wanted to cry but couldn't. She makes it known that when she looks at herself naked in the mirror she resembles someone in Auschwitz. Her boobs look like string beans, she says. She has a cup of cocoa and a banana and is full and cannot eat another bite.

My mother is the surviving parent of four. At times it looked like she would perish first. But she holds steadfast and is quietly strong. She will die last with no celebration.

***

The word "kindness" is nearly extinct in the English language. "Responsibility" and "accountability" are close behind.

Dear Cancel Culture, your assignment is to obliterate the easy, ineffective, ultimately, dismissive English word – closure ("conclusion" in Spanish) - terminate it with extreme prejudice. One definition of closure is "a feeling that an emotional or traumatic experience has been resolved." Taylor Swift sings about "closure."

When a parent, sibling, grandparent, husband, or wife is killed by a hit-and-run driver, blown to pieces in Afghanistan, or dies on the operating table following a butt-cheek implant gone wrong, the chuckling, gab-festing news anchors take time out from trading snarky put downs with the sportscaster over the local team losing, to sharing jokes with the weatherperson regarding the town's run of thirty days over a hundred degrees - to putting on a straight face.

The newsreader shifts down a few gears – there's a pause, it's serious, something important is about to be read - to warn the viewer that the following B-roll may contain images that will ruin their Pollo Loco take-out or Papa John's delivery. The video begins with the field reporter speaking solemnly over footage of dozens of candles, teddy bears, and balloons at the site commemorating a pedestrian getting nailed by a speeding drunk driver at two in the morning. Or it is the procession of military and official vehicles behind the hearse on the way to the Veterans Cemetery, then the close-up of the United States flag being tightly folded and handed to the adult survivor in the family, or perhaps the protest by women standing outside a cosmetic surgery clinic at the local strip mall.

There are sound bites from family members, co-workers, local and governmental officials (police, fire, military). At the end of the ninety-second video grab, the field reporter assures the viewer that the shock, the upheaval, the sadness, the absence, will be remedied soon by this phenomenon called "closure."

"Whew," says the viewer. "That was close." Back to the chicken and pizza.

The television watcher is sold the goods: the hundreds of candles, the oddly-folded flag placed in the lap of the survivor, the city or county official assuring the protestors that something will be done by somebody other than the group with misspelled placards. There's a sigh of relief. Ah, "closure." These are the moments that secure local Emmys for the newsrooms and ramp up their ratings.

But, after the microphone, video camera, and lights are put back in the truck and the field reporter and cameraperson drive away, back to the studio, to edit the tidy, minute-plus story, all the family, friends, and co-workers have are hazy memories, tattered personal items – a ring, a baseball mitt, a plaque, photographs, perhaps a film or video home movies, or maybe a few cell phone texts.

The people who remain are interviewed by police or attend religious services or go to the party that celebrates the dead with stories, food and drink, what they call a Celebration of Life.

An emotional or traumatic experience has not been resolved for the persons involved with or connected to the deceased. People have to go back to work. People have to take care of the family. People have to serve the country. Has anyone said "closure" except those in the newsroom, with such conviction?

As a high school student, I watched the Vietnam War unfold every evening on Walter Cronkite's report – soldiers barely older than me were dying daily in combat. There were leaders (John and Robert Kennedy, Dr. Martin Luther King, Malcolm

X) assassinated, sports teams in plane crashes, young children succumbing to cancer.

It was always someone else.

I watched the spouses, parents, children, and friends react with tears or stand there, stoic and silent. Jackie Kennedy wore her husband's blood for a day. I studied the facial expressions, posture, and conduct of the survivors. The television screen projected a sort of theatre.

This was an unreality brought into my home, a mourning I did not want to be part of. I was always relieved that death was happening elsewhere, to someone else, affecting other people – until it happened to me and my family and friends.

Thursday, June 29, 1978: I free-lanced for magazines and was transcribing an interview I had recently conducted with comedy actor Chevy Chase. I shared an apartment in Westwood with my father, actor Bob Crane, who was in the midst of a brutal divorce with my stepmother. My father, our Willy Loman, was on the road performing a play.

That afternoon I drove my grandmother, Rose (my father's mother), to Tarzana to visit her ex-daughter-in-law, Anne (my mother), her husband, Chuck (my stepfather), my two sisters, Debbie and Karen, and my other grandmother, Ellen. We pulled up in front of my mother and stepfather's home. Chuck, who had one of the greatest smiles, somberly directed me to his office phone to call my father's attorney.

"There's a rumor your dad's been shot," said Lloyd Vaughn, from his Beverly Hills office. "I'm flying to Phoenix. Do you want to go?"

I told everyone assembled in the kitchen. My father's mother screamed. My sisters immediately began to desperately weep. Chuck's smile would be absent for many days ahead.

When Vaughn and I landed in Phoenix, we were met at the airport by Scottsdale Police Department Officer Barry Vassall. On our way to the crime scene in Scottsdale, Vassall turned to us and said in a law enforcement monotone: "Gentlemen, I've got to inform you that Mr. Crane is deceased." My father hadn't been shot, he had been bludgeoned to death in the apartment the theatre had supplied to him.

That night, Vaughn and I checked into a motel. I called my family. Chuck was calm and quiet. I told him that my father - his wife's ex-husband - my sisters' father and my grandmother's son, was now dead.

There were more screams and wailing in the background when they looked at Chuck's expression. I sat by the motel pool in the oppressive heat and drank beer, numb.

The lives of my family members had changed forever – no more movie excursions with his son, me, visits with his ex-wife and her new husband, no more dinners with his daughters, shopping trips with his mother. No more laughter. No more fun with my father.

All of our former life gone.

The following year, Chuck bought season tickets to the Dodgers to get the family together and out of the house. Chuck and I grew closer. Yet, my mother, sisters, grandmothers, and Chuck, never had that 'hold hands' around the dining room table and talk about how Bob's - dad's - death had affected everyone.

It had, indeed, affected everyone–profoundly. My parents were small town Connecticut people, lower middle-class, people who didn't attend college but who went to work, got married and had children.

That's what you did in the Fifties. You didn't talk about it. You just did it.

Sixteen years later, the prime suspect, John Carpenter (not the filmmaker) went to trial and was found not guilty of the murder of my father. The case remains open and quite cold to this day. I realize it will never be solved in the traditional sense of the meaning. But I know who murdered my father.

In the decades since my father's murder, he has missed marriages, grandchildren, great grandchildren, divorces, careers, deaths - life - perhaps of more interest, laser discs, cds, dvds, hundreds of television series, innovative film technology, computers, cell phones, and his back room that he loved so much.

Life goes on but my father's life doesn't, except in TV reruns.

I think about my father almost every day. I dream about him occasionally. I wonder whether he would have made it to his nineties like my mother and stepfather did. I wonder whether he would have remarried, worked steadily, and attended celebrity autograph shows. I wonder how he would have aged – appearance, health, energy, and balance. I wonder whether his sense of humor would have remained intact.

I wonder how our friendship would have deepened with age.

My sisters and I missed out on hours and hours of conversations where we could have heard of his life experience and, ultimately, decide whether we wanted to emulate him or not. One sister has run from his history, the other sister pretends he is still alive, and I am in the middle writing it down, what I can remember and what makes sense to me.

Now, I know what death entails, how a family member dying stokes the family to become stronger or fall apart. There have been tears and laughter since my father died. My stepfather was a saint who held our family together as well as he could.

I cringe when news stories come on and are neatly tied together at the end of the report with that magical ribbon and bow – the word "closure" – as if a death has been filed, stacked, alphabetized, put away, out of sight, out of mind. The word is condescending, it is patronizing because there is no closure. Ever.

In the four decades since my father's murder, I've never settled into, or gotten used to his absence. I've never had the feeling that the emotional or traumatic experience of his death has been resolved.

Cancel *closure*.

My UnHollywood Family

My UnHollywood Family

My UnHollywood Family

About the Author

Robert Crane is the co-author of twelve books including *Crane: Sex, Celebrity, and My Father's Unsolved Murder*, *My Life as a Mankiewicz*, *Bruce Dern: A Memoir*, *SCTV: Behind the Scenes and Beyond* Where the Buses Run: Stories. Crane contributed to Playboy for twenty years and co-wrote the Fox Television film *Hostage for a Day* directed by John Candy.

About the Editor

Theresa Griffin Kennedy was born in Baker, Oregon and has lived in Portland, Oregon since she was eight-months-old. She is a writer of creative nonfiction, poetry, literary fiction in the genre of domestic noir, and crime history. She works as a freelance editor and is the publisher and editor of *Oregon Greystone Press*. In 2013 Kennedy completed a masters degree in *Adult Education, Leadership and Policy*, and in 2014, a masters certificate in *Teaching Adult Learners*. Kennedy is an advocate for prison reform through education, literacy and creative writing. She has been published in literary reviews, magazines, newspapers, several anthologies and in online news sources. Kennedy is the author of six books, including *Blue Reverie in Smoke: Collected Poems 2001-2016, Burnside Field Lizard and Select-*

ed Stories, Talionic Night in Portland: A Love Story, Beyond Where the Buses Run: Stories, and *Lost Restaurants of Portland, Oregon*. Kennedy is hard at work on her second novel, *The Angry Garbageman of Thurman Street*. She is married to Don DuPay, a writer, author, and a retired homicide detective who worked with PPB from 1961-1978.

Printed in the USA
CPSIA information can be obtained
at www.ICGtesting.com
LVHW021238081024
793246LV00013B/658